DATE DUE

MY 30 '94			
JE 17 '94			
NO 10 '94			
DE 23 '94			
MY 12 '95			
NO 27 '95			
MY 27 '97			
AP 27 '98			
DE 19 0			
NO 20 03			
NO 16 04			
DE 8 04			
MY 17 '05			

DEMCO 38-296

p. 73, 38

ENVIRONMENTAL HEALTH

THE ENCYCLOPEDIA OF
HEALTH

MEDICAL ISSUES

Dale C. Garell, M.D. • General Editor

ENVIRONMENTAL HEALTH

LaVonne Carlson-Finnerty

Introduction by C. Everett Koop, M.D., Sc.D.

former Surgeon General, U. S. Public Health Service

CHELSEA HOUSE PUBLISHERS

New York • Philadelphia

TH *is to provide general information in*
psychology, and related medical issues.
The titles in this series are ... *ed to take the place of the professional*
advice of a physician or other health care professional.

CHELSEA HOUSE PUBLISHERS
EDITORIAL DIRECTOR   Richard Rennert
EXECUTIVE MANAGING EDITOR   Karyn Gullen Browne
COPY CHIEF   Robin James
PICTURE EDITOR   Adrian G. Allen
ART DIRECTOR   Robert Mitchell
MANUFACTURING DIRECTOR   Gerald Levine
PRODUCTION COORDINATOR   Marie Claire Cebrián-Ume

The Encyclopedia of Health
SENIOR EDITOR   Don Nardo

Staff for ENVIRONMENTAL HEALTH
EDITORIAL ASSISTANT   Mary B. Sisson
PICTURE RESEARCHER   Sandy Jones
DESIGNER   M. Cambraia Magalhães

Copyright © 1994 by Chelsea House Publishers, a division of Main Line Book Co. All
rights reserved. Printed and bound in the United States of America.

First Printing
1   3   5   7   9   8   6   4   2

Library of Congress Cataloging-in-Publication Data

Carlson-Finnerty, LaVonne.
   Environmental health / LaVonne Carlson-Finnerty.
      p. cm.—(The Encyclopedia of health. Medical issues)
   Includes bibliographical references and index.
Summary: Examines the issues and concerns of environmental pollution and hazards.
ISBN 0-7910-0082-6
      0-7910-0519-4 (pbk.)
   1. Environmental health—Juvenile literature. [1. Environmental health. 2. Pollution.]
I. Title. II. Series.   93-20245
RA566.235.C27 1993   CIP
616.9'8—dc20   AC

CONTENTS

THE ENCYCLOPEDIA OF
H E A L T H

THE HEALTHY BODY

The Circulatory System
Dental Health
The Digestive System
The Endocrine System
Exercise
Genetics & Heredity
The Human Body: An Overview
Hygiene
The Immune System
Memory & Learning
The Musculoskeletal System
The Nervous System
Nutrition
The Reproductive System
The Respiratory System
The Senses
Sleep
Speech & Hearing
Sports Medicine
Vision
Vitamins & Minerals

THE LIFE CYCLE

Adolescence
Adulthood
Aging
Childhood
Death & Dying
The Family
Friendship & Love
Pregnancy & Birth

MEDICAL ISSUES

Careers in Health Care
Environmental Health
Folk Medicine
Health Care Delivery
Holistic Medicine
Medical Ethics
Medical Fakes & Frauds
Medical Technology
Medicine & the Law
Occupational Health
Public Health

PSYCHOLOGICAL DISORDERS AND THEIR TREATMENT

Anxiety & Phobias
Child Abuse
Compulsive Behavior
Delinquency & Criminal Behavior
Depression
Diagnosing & Treating Mental Illness
Eating Habits & Disorders
Learning Disabilities
Mental Retardation
Personality Disorders
Schizophrenia
Stress Management
Suicide

MEDICAL DISORDERS AND THEIR TREATMENT

AIDS
Allergies
Alzheimer's Disease
Arthritis
Birth Defects
Cancer
The Common Cold
Diabetes
Emergency Medicine
Gynecological Disorders
Headaches
The Hospital
Kidney Disorders
Medical Diagnosis
The Mind-Body Connection
Mononucleosis and Other Infectious Diseases
Nuclear Medicine
Organ Transplants
Pain
The Physically Challenged
Poisons & Toxins
Prescription & OTC Drugs
Sexually Transmitted Diseases
Skin Disorders
Stroke & Heart Disease
Substance Abuse
Tropical Medicine

PREVENTION AND EDUCATION: THE KEYS TO GOOD HEALTH

C. Everett Koop, M.D., Sc.D.
former Surgeon General,
U.S. Public Health Service

The issue of health education has received particular attention in recent years because of the presence of AIDS in the news. But our response to this particular tragedy points up a number of broader issues that doctors, public health officials, educators, and the public face. In particular, it points up the necessity for sound health education for citizens of all ages.

Over the past 25 years this country has been able to bring about dramatic declines in the death rates for heart disease, stroke, accidents, and for people under the age of 45, cancer. Today, Americans generally eat better and take better care of themselves than ever before. Thus, with the help of modern science and technology, they have a better chance of surviving serious—even catastrophic—illnesses. That's the good news.

But, like every phonograph record, there's a flip side, and one with special significance for young adults. According to a report issued in 1979 by Dr. Julius Richmond, my predecessor as Surgeon General, Americans aged 15 to 24 had a higher death rate in 1979 than they did 20 years earlier. The causes: violent death and injury, alcohol and drug abuse, unwanted pregnancies, and sexually transmitted diseases. Adolescents are particularly vulnerable because they are beginning to explore their own sexuality and perhaps to experiment with drugs. The need for educating young people is critical, and the price of neglect is high.

Yet even for the population as a whole, our health is still far from what it could be. Why? A 1974 Canadian government report attributed all death and disease to four broad elements: inadequacies in the health care system, behavioral factors or unhealthy life-styles, environmental hazards, and human biological factors.

To be sure, there are diseases that are still beyond the control of even our advanced medical knowledge and techniques. And despite yearnings that are as old as the human race itself, there is no "fountain of youth" to ward off aging and death. Still, there is a solution to many of the problems that undermine sound health. In a word, that solution is prevention. Prevention, which includes health promotion and education, saves lives, improves the quality of life, and in the long run, saves money.

In the United States, organized public health activities and preventive medicine have a long history. Important milestones in this country or foreign breakthroughs adopted in the United States include the improvement of sanitary procedures and the development of pasteurized milk in the late 19th century and the introduction in the mid-20th century of effective vaccines against polio, measles, German measles, mumps, and other once-rampant diseases. Internationally, organized public health efforts began on a wide-scale basis with the International Sanitary Conference of 1851, to which 12 nations sent representatives. The World Health Organization, founded in 1948, continues these efforts under the aegis of the United Nations, with particular emphasis on combating communicable diseases and the training of health care workers.

Despite these accomplishments, much remains to be done in the field of prevention. For too long, we have had a medical care system that is science- and technology-based, focused, essentially, on illness and mortality. It is now patently obvious that both the social and the economic costs of such a system are becoming insupportable.

Implementing prevention—and its corollaries, health education and pro- motion—is the job of several groups of people.

First, the medical and scientific professions need to continue basic scien- tific research, and here we are making considerable progress. But increased concern with prevention will also have a decided impact on how primary care doctors practice medicine. With a shift to health-based rather than morbidity- based medicine, the role of the "new physician" will include a healthy dose of patient education.

Second, practitioners of the social and behavioral sciences—psycholo- gists, economists, city planners—along with lawyers, business leaders, and government officials—must solve the practical and ethical dilemmas con- fronting us: poverty, crime, civil rights, literacy, education, employment, housing, sanitation, environmental protection, health care delivery systems, and so forth. All of these issues affect public health.

Third is the public at large. We'll consider that very important group in a moment.

Fourth, and the linchpin in this effort, is the public health profession—doctors, epidemiologists, teachers—who must harness the professional expertise of the first two groups and the common sense and cooperation of the third, the public. They must define the problems statistically and qualitatively and then help us set priorities for finding the solutions.

To a very large extent, improving those statistics is the responsibility of every individual. So let's consider more specifically what the role of the individual should be and why health education is so important to that role. First, and most obvious, individuals can protect themselves from illness and injury and thus minimize their need for professional medical care. They can eat nutritious food; get adequate exercise; avoid tobacco, alcohol, and drugs; and take prudent steps to avoid accidents. The proverbial "apple a day keeps the doctor away" is not so far from the truth, after all.

Second, individuals should actively participate in their own medical care. They should schedule regular medical and dental checkups. Should they develop an illness or injury, they should know when to treat themselves and when to seek professional help. To gain the maximum benefit from any medical treatment that they do require, individuals must become partners in that treatment. For instance, they should understand the effects and side effects of medications. I counsel young physicians that there is no such thing as too much information when talking with patients. But the corollary is the patient must know enough about the nuts and bolts of the healing process to understand what the doctor is telling him or her. That is at least partially the patient's responsibility.

Education is equally necessary for us to understand the ethical and public policy issues in health care today. Sometimes individuals will encounter these issues in making decisions about their own treatment or that of family members. Other citizens may encounter them as jurors in medical malpractice cases. But we all become involved, indirectly, when we elect our public officials, from school board members to the president. Should surrogate parenting be legal? To what extent is drug testing desirable, legal, or necessary? Should there be public funding for family planning, hospitals, various types of medical research, and other medical care for the indigent? How should we allocate scant technological resources, such as kidney dialysis and organ transplants? What is the proper role of government in protecting the rights of patients?

What are the broad goals of public health in the United States today? In 1980, the Public Health Service issued a report aptly entitled *Promoting Health—Preventing Disease: Objectives for the Nation.* This report expressed its goals in terms of mortality and in terms of intermediate goals in education and health improvement. It identified 15 major concerns: controlling high blood pressure; improving family planning; improving pregnancy care and infant health; increasing the rate of immunization; controlling sexually transmitted diseases; controlling the presence of toxic agents and radiation in the environment; improving occupational safety and health; preventing accidents; promoting water fluoridation and dental health; controlling infectious diseases; decreasing smoking; decreasing alcohol and drug abuse; improving nutrition; promoting physical fitness and exercise; and controlling stress and violent behavior.

For healthy adolescents and young adults (ages 15 to 24), the specific goal was a 20% reduction in deaths, with a special focus on motor vehicle injuries and alcohol and drug abuse. For adults (ages 25 to 64), the aim was 25% fewer deaths, with a concentration on heart attacks, strokes, and cancers.

Smoking is perhaps the best example of how individual behavior can have a direct impact on health. Today, cigarette smoking is recognized as the single most important preventable cause of death in our society. It is responsible for more cancers and more cancer deaths than any other known agent; is a prime risk factor for heart and blood vessel disease, chronic bronchitis, and emphysema; and is a frequent cause of complications in pregnancies and of babies born prematurely, underweight, or with potentially fatal respiratory and cardiovascular problems.

Since the release of the Surgeon General's first report on smoking in 1964, the proportion of adult smokers has declined substantially, from 43% in 1965 to 30.5% in 1985. Since 1965, 37 million people have quit smoking. Although there is still much work to be done if we are to become a "smoke-free society," it is heartening to note that public health and public education efforts—such as warnings on cigarette packages and bans on broadcast advertising—have already had significant effects.

In 1835, Alexis de Tocqueville, a French visitor to America, wrote, "In America the passion for physical well-being is general." Today, as then, health and fitness are front-page items. But with the greater scientific and technological resources now available to us, we are in a far stronger position to make good health care available to everyone. And with the greater technological threats to us as we approach the 21st century, the need to do so is more urgent than ever before. Comprehensive information about basic biology, preventive medicine, medical and surgical treatments, and related ethical and public policy issues can help you arm yourself with the knowledge you need to be healthy throughout your life.

FOREWORD

Dale C. Garell, M.D.

Advances in our understanding of health and disease during the 20th century have been truly remarkable. Indeed, it could be argued that modern health care is one of the greatest accomplishments in all of human history. In the early 20th century, improvements in sanitation, water treatment, and sewage disposal reduced death rates and increased longevity. Previously untreatable illnesses can now be managed with antibiotics, immunizations, and modern surgical techniques. Discoveries in the fields of immunology, genetic diagnosis, and organ transplantation are revolutionizing the prevention and treatment of disease. Modern medicine is even making inroads against cancer and heart disease, two of the leading causes of death in the United States.

Although there is much to be proud of, medicine continues to face enormous challenges. Science has vanquished diseases such as smallpox and polio, but new killers, most notably AIDS, confront us. Moreover, we now victimize ourselves with what some have called "diseases of choice," or those brought on by drug and alcohol abuse, bad eating habits, and mismanagement of the stresses and strains of contemporary life. The very technology that is doing so much to prolong life has brought with it previously unimaginable ethical dilemmas related to issues of death and dying. The rising cost of health care is a matter of central concern to us all. And violence in the form of automobile accidents, homicide, and suicide remains the major killer of young adults.

In the past, most people were content to leave health care and medical treatment in the hands of professionals. But since the 1960s, the consumer of medical care—that is, the patient—has assumed an increasingly central role in the management of his or her own health. There has also been a new emphasis placed on prevention: People are recognizing that their own actions can help prevent many of the conditions that have caused death and disease in the past. This accounts for the growing commitment to good nutrition and regular exercise, for the increasing number of people who are choosing not to smoke, and for a new moderation in people's drinking habits.

People want to know more about themselves and their own health. They are curious about their body: its anatomy, physiology, and biochemistry. They want to keep up with rapidly evolving medical technologies and procedures. They are willing to educate themselves about common disorders and diseases so that they can be full partners in their own health care.

THE ENCYCLOPEDIA OF HEALTH is designed to provide the basic knowledge that readers will need if they are to take significant responsibility for their own health. It is also meant to serve as a frame of reference for further study and exploration. The encyclopedia is divided into five subsections: The Healthy Body; The Life Cycle; Medical Disorders & Their Treatment; Psychological Disorders & Their Treatment; and Medical Issues. For each topic covered by the encyclopedia, we present the essential facts about the relevant biology; the symptoms, diagnosis, and treatment of common diseases and disorders; and ways in which you can prevent or reduce the severity of health problems when that is possible. The encyclopedia also projects what may lie ahead in the way of future treatment or prevention strategies.

The broad range of topics and issues covered in the encyclopedia reflects that human health encompasses physical, psychological, social, environmental, and spiritual well-being. Just as the mind and the body are inextricably linked, so, too, is the individual an integral part of the wider world that comprises his or her family, society, and environment. To discuss health in its broadest aspect it is necessary to explore the many ways in which it is connected to such fields as law, social science, public policy, economics, and even religion. And so, the encyclopedia is meant to be a bridge between science, medical technology, the world at large, and you. I hope that it will inspire you to pursue in greater depth particular areas of interest and that you will take advantage of the suggestions for further reading and the lists of resources and organizations that can provide additional information.

CHAPTER 1

ENVIRONMENTAL HEALTH: THE BIG PICTURE

Because pollutants and toxic materials cannot be confined within the borders of one nation, environmental health is a global problem.

Environmental health is a term that means many things to many people. *Webster's New Collegiate Dictionary* describes *health* as "freedom from physical disease or pain." But the word *environmental* introduces an entirely different perspective on health. Primarily, environmental health refers to the well-being that individuals experience when their surroundings are clean and safe. Usually, people feel no concern about environmental health until they suffer effects of environmental illness, which usually occurs when people's surroundings have become unsafe.

Some causes of illness are clearly recognized as originating from a person's environment. For example, lung disease caused by cigarette smoking is an environmental illness because a smoker regularly fills his or her immediate environment with harmful tobacco smoke. In the United States, smoking is listed as the top cause of preventable death. If smokers quit the habit and thereby improve their immediate environments by eliminating tobacco smoke, they can greatly reduce their risk of suffering from heart and lung diseases.

Many sources of environmental illness are not as easy to recognize or control as smoking, yet these threats fill many people's surroundings on a daily basis. Most people tend to judge the safety of the environment in terms of their immediate or local surroundings. If they do not see health hazards in their home or work place, they usually rest assured that their environment is safe. However, their environment may contain unseen and undiscovered health threats. For instance, many people assume that their water is safe as long as it looks clear and does not taste strange. Yet their water may contain chemicals that, over many years, could cause illness or abnormal physical changes.

Many other seemingly harmless aspects of local environments may eventually prove hazardous or even lethal. For example, certain food products, construction materials, and even some indoor ventilation systems can pose unseen threats.

The Global Environment

A number of larger-scale health hazards also exist. On a worldwide scale, the term *environmental health* applies to the health of the global environment itself. In this sense, *environment* describes the condition of the entire earth. The land and sky could be viewed as the floor below and the ceiling above a home that all people share. As technology brings people around the world closer together, it also brings a growing awareness of the entire planet's health. And as scientists learn more about the earth as a whole, they are beginning to recognize that its health also affects the health of every individual. When the earth becomes environmentally damaged, or "diseased," so do many individuals.

There are many ways that one type of environmental damage can create a health threat to both individuals and the world at large. For example, an individual may drive a car that uses excessive amounts of fuel. As the fuel burns, it releases gases that pollute the air. This polluted air makes breathing more difficult for those people who live

In many underdeveloped countries, there is a desperate need for adequate sanitation to control diseases. These children scavenge through the garbage floating in an open sewer.

in the city where the car is driven. But the polluted air also accumulates, along with other air pollution, and gets carried by the wind to more distant areas, including the countryside. The polluted air also collects in clouds that eventually produce rain, releasing the pollution into the land and rivers below. This pollution enters the food and water supply of many people around the world, including the driver of the car that initially used too much fuel.

The effects of unclean water and air show themselves in many ways. Indirectly, they may damage food crops, which can lead to starvation. Directly, as more pollution collects inside people's bodies, they may gradually become ill. Pollutants may cause a wide range of individual discomforts, from feeling a little irritable to dying from a long-term illness.

Cancer is among the most common illnesses that may result from unsafe environmental conditions. Cancer is a general name used to describe many varieties of an illness that involves accelerated cell growth. Normally, the body has a system of replacing old cells with new ones, but occasionally this system goes awry. When the body replaces cells in a specific area at an accelerated rate, this abnormal growth may create a tumor. It can become dangerous if it continues to grow and overtake healthily functioning areas. Substances which lead to cancer after repeated exposure to them are called *carcinogens.*

Environmental hazards come from many sources and create a number of effects, many of which are not as threatening as cancer. And not all environmental illnesses are caused by modern by-products of technology, such as toxic chemicals. Although air pollution has increased dramatically in the past few centuries, other forms of contamination have existed at least as long as humans have.

Environmental Hygiene in the Past

Humans have known the importance of respecting the environment's natural balance since the days of the earliest tribal cultures. These groups often used periodic migration as a way of ensuring a clean environment. They would build encampments near a clean water supply and remain there until the area had become contaminated with

Factory pollution drains into the Pecos River near Carlsbad, New Mexico.

human waste. Then the tribe would move to other, cleaner surroundings with a safe water supply and uncontaminated land.

Even in ancient times, people had some sense of hygiene and the importance of a clean environment. As early as 2000 B.C., Babylonian laws forbade the sale of contaminated grain. The ancient Greeks, including the philosophers Plato and Hippocrates, recognized the link between disease and an overcrowded environment. The Hebrews and Romans also showed concern for private and public sanitation. In fact, to keep their living areas clean, the Romans built a famous system of aqueducts and sewers, some of which are still in use today. The first laws prohibiting excessive coal burning went into effect in England in 1273, with a punishment of death in at least one case.

In the 17th and 18th centuries, the Industrial Revolution brought new levels of contamination to many areas of the world. As more people moved into cities to work in the factories, they added to ever-growing amounts of waste. At the same time, living conditions began to decline due to overcrowding. Poor sanitation facilities in overcrowded cities increased the spread of communicable diseases, including tuberculosis, a contagious lung disease.

Meanwhile, inventors began to develop new devices for sanitary engineering and scientists gained an understanding of how disease and the environment interact. In the mid-19th century, the French scientist Louis Pasteur introduced the germ theory of disease, the idea that much disease is caused by microorganisms that invade larger organisms. The German bacteriologist Robert Koch further contributed to this hypothesis, suggesting that these microorganisms spread communicable diseases.

Yet another type of health threat—the by-products of industry— began to pollute the environment to a much greater degree than human waste. In the early phases of the Industrial Revolution, factories were the main source of air pollution. Toxic metals and chemicals that resulted from industrial processes spread rapidly through the air and water. As the residue of coal collected in the air, the sky over many large European and American cities began to appear black with pollution. On several occasions in the 1940s and 1950s, London smog landed thousands of people in hospitals, with hundreds dying within a period of a few days. Such incidents alerted people to the dangers of air pollution, and in time the use of coal as a fuel in both houses and factories declined. However, air pollution caused by power plants and motor vehicle emissions became an increasingly serious problem in the second half of the 20th century.

Despite the realization that air pollution could make many people ill, some of the excesses of the Industrial Revolution continue today. Many individuals and industries continue to overconsume natural resources and pollute their surroundings without regard for negative side effects. However, other individuals and organizations have worked to improve the environment. For example, in 1962, Rachel Carson's controversial book *Silent Spring* made many people aware of a number of serious environmental health threats. The widely read book describes the side effects of environmental pollutants and poisons, particularly the insecticide DDT.

The discovery of other similar problems had already begun to make people doubt the judgment of scientists and medical authorities. In 1959, the drug thalidomide, often prescribed to pregnant mothers, was discovered to be a teratogen, a substance that causes malformations in offspring as they grow inside the womb. Some people began to distrust

This antismoking poster, drawn by a 12-year-old New York student, parodies a popular cigarette advertisement and was displayed in the New York City subway system.

Smoking kills more Americans each year than alcohol, cocaine, crack, heroin, homicide, suicide, car accidents, fires, and AIDS combined.

doctors and chemical cures and to question the use of chemicals both inside and outside the human body.

In the United States, Massachusetts was the first state to take legal action to ensure environmental health. In 1848, the state made plans to survey its sanitation facilities and two years later proposed the creation of a health department to regulate state standards. Many of these standards have since been adopted by other states and are still followed today.

Federal authorities were much slower to act. Until growing numbers of people became aware of possible health threats from their environment at large, the federal government did little to ensure environmental safety. A major step toward setting environmental guidelines appeared with the National Environmental Policy Act of 1969. This law requires federal agencies to account for the environmental impact of any program that might affect the environment before such programs take effect. In many cases, alternative plans have proven safer for communities as well as the environment at large.

In 1963, the United States Congress developed the Clean Air Act, creating a regulatory system to maintain standards for the improvement of air quality. However, the law had little impact until Congress amended the law in 1970. At that time, it required that cars emit far less pollutants, a standard that forced automobile manufacturers to install catalytic converters, devices that convert automobile exhaust into less harmful products. Today, most cities are cleaner than they were in the 1970s, yet the number of cars on the roads continues to increase by almost 5% annually. In 1990, Congress adopted dramatic amendments to the Clean Air Act that concentrate on cleaning up a wide variety of contaminants found in fuel. Meanwhile, many developing countries, in an effort to catch up with industrialized nations, are rapidly increasing the number of their roads and vehicles, often without putting fuel safeguards in place.

Since 1970, many more U.S. laws have been introduced with the intent of reducing pollutants and hazardous substances. Among the major laws are the Clean Water Act, the Safe Drinking Water Act, and the Resource Conservation and Recovery Act, which regulates the disposal of solid waste. The Comprehensive Environmental Response,

This potash mine in southeastern New Mexico spews pollutants into the air, where they are carried to other regions of the country.

Compensation, and Liability Act, often referred to as Superfund, was adopted in 1980 to oversee the disposal of hazardous waste which was improperly handled in the past. Many more laws have been designed to prevent the spread of toxic substances and to regulate other aspects of environmental health, such as wildlife and habitat protection, and nuclear power and energy production.

The Environmental Protection Agency, or EPA, is the primary enforcer of these laws. This federal agency is responsible for overseeing the long-term health and safety of the environment. Among its many responsibilities, it attempts to measure and control the production and disposal of thousands of unhealthy substances. The EPA often encounters criticism for its lack of efficiency and enforcement, but EPA officials contend that the agency has a vast number of individual duties and, like other governmental agencies, has limited funds.

These factors sometimes make environmental laws difficult to enforce. Nevertheless, these laws can be used as important weapons within the legal system. Once a law exists, any organization which does not follow them can be taken to court. For instance, if a corporation refuses to follow set standards, it can be sued in court and then forced to comply with regulations. In this way, communities can use federal laws to protect their resources on a local level.

While federal, state, and local governments have made efforts to protect the environment in recent decades, government officials say that individuals must also assume some measure of responsibility. This responsibility begins with people understanding the problems so that they can help federal and local officials implement solutions. The key to controlling environmental threats is understanding that they endanger everyone equally and are, therefore, everyone's problem.

CHAPTER 2

THE
LIMITS OF LAND

In this Maryland landfill, the U.S. Department of Agriculture is trying to bury a mixture of sewage and wood chips that will enrich the soil. But as available land becomes more scarce, burying garbage may not be a practical solution.

People in many ancient civilizations believed that everything in the universe consisted of either earth, water, or air. When they looked around them, these three elements seemed to make up the basis of their existence. Although modern science has shown that everything consists of atoms, particles too small to be seen, many people can relate to the age-old feeling that they are surrounded by land, sea, and sky. Because people live on land, they feel a comfortable closeness with the earth. And because they have such close contact with land, it is the element that most clearly and immediately shows signs of destruction.

The Importance of Plants

The word *land* means much more than the earth underfoot. It involves all of the life that land supports. The land in each geographic area takes hundreds of centuries to evolve, gradually developing its own unique types of plants and animals. Specific weather and soil conditions slowly form a perfectly balanced environment that supports many interdependent life forms. The plants and animals in a given area evolve into a delicately balanced environment referred to as an *ecosystem.*

Rainforests are an example of highly evolved ecosystems. These forests thrive on land that is naturally ideal for tropical plants, which grow well in wet climates without rich soil. Although these areas look luxuriantly green with many plants, the soil is not rich enough to support nutrient-hungry grain crops or grasslands. Topsoil in the tropics does not contain enough nutrients to grow more than a one-year supply of grass or grain. Yet many newcomers to the tropical forest do not understand these limitations. They have introduced farming techniques that irreparably damage these ecosystems, which took centuries to form.

Often the type of food raised in a certain area is not appropriate for that region's type of soil and climate. Resources are often misused and wasted when people raise crops or livestock on land which is not capable of sustaining them. Cattle ranching in the South American tropics is an example of this misuse of land. In order to provide meat for people in the Northern Hemisphere, 4 billion cattle, sheep, pigs, and other animals must be fed on grassland where tropical forests recently thrived. This grazing crop creates a dramatic strain in regions of the world where the land is not naturally prepared to raise cattle. In just a few seasons, the land is no longer able to support livestock ranching.

Modern farming practices—the use of fertilizers, pesticides, and lots of irrigation water—erode topsoil and may produce desertlike conditions on what was once fertile crop land.

The loss of forest land creates a serious problem referred to as deforestation, the process whereby native forests are cleared to introduce new crops or livestock. Once the centuries-old forest has been replaced with grass or grain which is used to feed cattle for one short season, the soil may not be rich enough to enable even the grass to grow back.

Further problems occur in these areas when rain washes over the bare, overgrazed hillsides, taking away the remaining rich topsoil and making the land even less susceptible to growing grass. The process whereby rain and wind carry away topsoil is called soil erosion. Areas with high erosion rates often correspond to areas with higher popula-

This hillside in New Mexico dramatically demonstrates the effects of soil erosion when the ground loses its protective covering of trees and vegetation.

tions because the most common cause of erosion is mismanagement of land by people. Following deforestation, overcultivation, and overgrazing, the land's biological productivity decreases, a process referred to as desertification. In extreme cases, once-fertile land becomes barren like a desert.

Photosynthesis

The loss of forest land affects people in many ways beyond decreasing the amount of land available for food growth. Forests have a less visible, but tremendously important, function: They take in stale air, purify it, and release clean air. All humans depend on oxygen to breathe and to live. For humans and other animals, carbon dioxide is unhealthy air, a waste product they exhale after breathing in fresh, healthy oxygen. Plants produce the clean oxygen that humans need through photosynthesis, a biological process that enables plants to absorb carbon dioxide and transform it into oxygen.

Tropical forests are responsible for much of the photosynthesis that occurs on earth. South America's Amazon rainforests produce approximately 40% of the earth's oxygen. Yet almost half of the world's original tropical rain forests have been destroyed by human activity. As humans destroy plants and trees to clear land for cattle and crops, fewer plants remain to do the work of cleaning air. Furthermore, when forests are cleared, the unwanted trees are burned, a practice that releases great quantities of carbon dioxide into the air. The problem worsens when growing numbers of livestock and humans add even more carbon dioxide to the air supply as they function on a daily basis. Forests and all the plants they contain are necessary to produce clean, cool air for life to continue, but by destroying forests, humans are hurting their own ability to breathe and to live.

Solid Wastes

At the same time that humans decrease the amount of land available for plants to provide fresh food and air, they are creating greater amounts of wastes that also take up space. Most solid wastes end up filling space on land in *landfills,* open sites where trash is dumped. Landfills create various types of health threats. The obvious problems of living near a dump site include dealing with litter, odors, and rodents. But the unseen effects produced by waste, and by landfills in particular, can be extremely dangerous because of the many toxic, but invisible, substances they release. These unseen substances harm humans if consumed in large amounts or over a long period of time.

One of these harmful substances, leachate, is formed when compounds created by the waste are carried away by rainwater that runs through a dump site. Some of these waste compounds contain toxic materials, especially those that come from metallic waste. As these toxic compounds wash away, they are carried with the rainwater into

Climate changes caused by atmospheric pollutants can bring about droughts that ruin crops.

the underground water supply. *Groundwater* is the water that runs in interconnecting pools deep below the earth's surface. Even a small amount of leachate can spread easily throughout this water supply. Many people use groundwater as their main source of drinking water and may not be aware that leachate has entered and polluted it.

A second toxic substance produced in landfills is methane, a gas created when bacteria decompose waste. Methane is combustible and sometimes explosive, and thus can cause fires and explosions if it seeps through the ground into nearby buildings within reach of flames. In addition, methane replaces oxygen in soil, thereby reducing the oxygen supply of the surrounding vegetation. Fortunately, more modern landfills are built with a lining that prevents methane and leachate from seeping into surrounding land. Additionally, they now include a system of checking for leaks and piping excessive levels of toxic gases to nearby wells where these substances can be cleaned for future use.

Despite these improvements, another problem remains: Many landfills are filling so fast that they will soon be required to close. For instance, the United States had approximately 20,000 landfills available for use in 1978, but that number dropped to 6,000 in 1988. By 2005 the remaining number of landfills will have decreased by 75%. Meanwhile, creating new landfills is difficult because disposal fees are so high. These fees result from the growing cost of insurance, audits, permits, improvements, and the expectation of future costs of closure and new construction.

Incineration

To help reduce the amount of space consumed by trash, many landfill facilities burn solid waste before it is dumped, a practice called incineration. This technique typically reduces the volume of solid waste by 90%, but the by-products of burning trash contain potential toxins, air and water pollution, and hazardous materials in bottom and fly ash. Bottom ash is waste that remains in incinerators after burning. The term *fly ash* refers to the lightweight particles produced from gaseous wastes called effluents.

Landfill sites for the burial of waste are now so rare that many urban areas must transport their garbage by barge to sites hundreds of miles away.

To prevent air pollution, the EPA now requires incinerator operators to monitor gases released when burning occurs. High-tech devices called scrubbers and sorters remove toxins from air as it leaves the smokestack. Government regulations are likely to become stricter as engineers find better ways to filter these toxins and avoid pollution.

Another, newer type of incinerator has been developed that generates energy from the trash it burns. Referred to both as resource recovery facilities and mass burn facilities, these incinerators burn at extremely high temperatures—between 1,300°F and 2,400°F. The energy released by this process can be used to heat nearby buildings or to generate electricity. A major drawback to using these high-tech incinerators is their high cost, sometimes priced at $150 million or more. However, over time these advanced versions of incinerators help pay for themselves. And as these methods develop and improve, their cost is likely to decrease.

Despite the improvement offered by mass burn facilities, their remaining ash still takes up 10% to 15% of the solid waste's original volume. Even more volume can be reduced with additional efforts to sort out all metal and glass before burning. Special incinerators called refuse-derived fuel facilities recycle almost all of their incinerated trash into electricity. These plants use a magnetic system to remove metallic materials and shredders to allow easy separation of glass from paper.

The United States generates some 160 million tons of solid waste annually and spends over $6 billion every year to handle trash. Remarkably, half of this trash is paper that could be recycled easily. As more people become aware of the damage caused by excess garbage and the benefits gained by conservation, the environment will become safer and healthier for people around the globe.

Nuclear Waste

Another type of waste, one which no one yet knows how to dispose of effectively, is nuclear waste, the radioactive by-product of nuclear weapons and power plants. When people hear the word *radiation,* they typically think of bombs or power facilities. But in fact, everything gives off radiation because everything consists of molecules and their invisibly small components, atoms. Atoms have been called the building blocks of matter, and everything that exists is made up of these tiny particles. Atoms do not actually contain matter. They are more like bundles of frantic motion, which constantly move and change. The energy caused by their ongoing changes creates light and particles. The particles interact to form matter. Yet the action produced by atoms and the matter they form creates different types of energy.

Radiation is produced when atoms release energy, which is then carried by electromagnetic waves of differing lengths. Each of these various wavelengths represents a different type of radiation. When discussing possibly harmful effects of radiation, experts define radiation by dividing it into two categories, ionizing and nonionizing. Nonionizing radiation is not considered harmful, but the level of energy in ionizing radiation is high enough to alter molecules that are vital to a living cell. This ability makes ionizing radiation harmful to living organisms. Ionizing radiation in small amounts does not seem harmful. However, the accumulated effect from a number of various sources may create severe health problems, including damaged cells, abnormal cell division, and genetic mutations. These can result in cancer or birth defects.

Often, a certain type of radioactive material affects certain parts of the body in specific ways. For example, iodine 131 tends to collect in the thyroid gland and ovaries and is especially threatening to young children. Strontium 90, a by-product of nuclear plants, collects in the bones, where it affects bone marrow and increases the threat of blood

The land may also be used to store low-level radioactive waste, though no one knows how long such sites can effectively contain radioactive leakage.

diseases such as leukemia. Another by-product of nuclear plants, cesium 137 tends to be absorbed by the kidneys, liver, and reproductive organs.

Nuclear Plants

There are more than 400 nuclear power plants operating around the world, including 100 in the United States. Each year, the average power plant produces approximately 450 pounds of plutonium, the highly toxic by-product of nuclear power. Combined, the world's nuclear power plants create over 70 tons of plutonium per year. In addition to these facilities, many countries now have weapons-related nuclear reactors which add to the nuclear waste problem. Underlying the growing amount of nuclear waste is the unanswered question: What should be done with the waste?

Although nuclear reactors and power plants have been operating for at least 40 years, no solution has yet been found to the problem of where to store nuclear waste. This waste is extremely lethal and durable. For example, the 70 tons of plutonium created each year has a *half-life* of 24,300 years. The term *half-life* refers to the amount of time it takes for one-half of the substance's radioactive atoms to disintegrate. While this decay process occurs, the 70 tons will remain dangerous to human health—for a half million years. One-millionth of a gram of plutonium—an amount invisible to the naked eye—can cause cancer if inhaled. One-thousandth of a gram can cause fibrosis, a condition characterized by a growth within tissue fiber, in the lungs and result in death within a few years. Yet these dangerous wastes reach thousands of people through improper storage and disposal practices.

The lack of proper storage for nuclear waste often allows these lethal substances to leak out into surrounding water and air, either by accident or, in some cases, by plan. Nuclear power plants produce radioactive effluents from burned fuel that may escape into the air, where they can be carried to thousands of people in the surrounding areas and beyond. In addition, much high-level radioactive waste is stored in tanks of water, awaiting a permanent storage place, which at this time does not exist.

Lower-level radioactive wastes are often buried in shallow storage tanks. However, this highly corrosive material can penetrate storage containers and seep throughout the surrounding land. The greatest threat from this process occurs when the waste reaches underground water supplies. Once it enters groundwater, it may spread into drinking water for hundreds of miles around. It may also wash into rivers and lakes and from there to the sea, also corrupting plants and animals so that the radiation spreads to whoever eats the crops and livestock.

Presently, solutions to nuclear storage and disposal problems seem limited. For many years, the most popular idea has been to store the wastes deep underground, at a depth of approximately 1,000 to 4,000 feet below the land's surface. A site with underlying volcanic ash in the southern New Mexico desert had been chosen for this storage facility until recent findings revealed that this area was prone to volcanic eruptions and shifting along a fault line. The site no longer appears secure for storage of deadly nuclear materials.

Accidents and Other Dangers

Accidents in nuclear power plants are also a major source of exposure to nuclear wastes. The most famous and most severe nuclear power accidents have occurred in recent years. The Three Mile Island plant in Pennsylvania leaked radiation in 1979, and the Chernobyl plant in the former Soviet Union leaked radiation in 1986. Similar catastrophes have the potential of occurring daily in nuclear power plants throughout the United States and around the world. According to the *Critical Mass Energy Bulletin* of June/August 1989, a total of 2,940 mishaps were reported in 110 United States nuclear power plants in 1987. Often these accidents are caught in time to prevent catastrophe, yet many leaks occur that are not even reported.

After nuclear power plants operate for about 30 years, they lose their effectiveness and must be closed permanently. Closing a power plant presents a new problem. Because it remains contaminated, something must be done to contain its waste. Although scientists are not certain about what to do about this problem, they have basically three possibilities. First, they can immediately dismantle the reactor. Second,

THE POPULATION BOMB

The world is now home to approximately 5.2 billion people, a number that increases by 90 million people every year. At this rate, the world's population will reach 6 billion people by the year 2000, then almost double to 10 billion people by the year 2025. This rapid rate of increase has led experts to coin the phrase "population explosion." Based on these numbers environmentalists fear that the biggest problem facing the world and its inhabitants is overpopulation.

This rapidly expanding population presents various problems. In many parts of the world, food, water, shelter, employment, and education are already limited or completely inadequate for existing populations. Increasing the number of people will require additional amounts of these resources in the future and this demand will create even greater stress on the environment.

Stress on the environment hurts both the land and the people that depend on it. Overpopulation tends to push a region beyond its "carrying capacity," the long-term ability to support its inhabitants without damaging its economic and naturalresources. In recent years, many human needs arereaching beyond what the land is capable of producing. When a region exceeds its carrying capacity, one sign of excess stress is that more people begin to suffer. For example, in developing nations that experience environmental deterioration, widespread hunger and malnutrition become apparent.

Resources are increasingly shared on a global scale.But as worldwide population continues to grow, resources will become increasingly limited. For this reason, some experts fear that a population explosion could lead to desperate struggles for limited supplies of food and usable water.

they can wait several decades before dismantling it so that short-lived radioactive materials can dissipate somewhat. Third, they can entomb the reactor, encasing it permanently inside a concrete container. Although entombment sounds effective, this idea is almost impossible to carry out because the radioactive substances would last longer than any structure built around them. Dismantling the reactor presents a separate problem. Although high-level radiation can be removed, the plant would continue to contain low-level radiation, a type of contamination that is almost impossible to dispose of entirely.

Unfortunately, all of these methods are extremely expensive and none is entirely effective. In October 1989, the *New York Times* reported on the cleanup cost of one nuclear power plant in West Valley, New York. Although it closed in 1972, 10 years later the estimated cost to begin its cleanup was $400 million. By 1989, that cost had risen to $890 million, an amount which is likely to increase again before the project is complete. And this represents only one of many similar cases. By the year 2000, another 71 nuclear power plants are likely to close down around the world.

Despite the fearful outlook presented by growing amounts of nuclear and solid wastes, the hope remains that technology will offer new alternatives. While scientists search for more efficient energy alternatives and cleaner ways to dispose of wastes, individuals can help by decreasing the amount of refuse and energy they use.

CHAPTER 3

WATER: PLENTIFUL, BUT PURE?

*In Central Africa, a young boy leads a man
blinded by onchocerciasis, a disease caused by
a worm that thrives in river water. Worldwide, 20
million people suffer from this disease.*

Every living creature depends on water for survival. In fact, most of the human body is composed of water. And three-quarters of the earth's surface is covered by water. Yet, while water may seem like an infinite resource, in reality it is not. Most of it is in the oceans and is too salty for human use. Much of the remaining water is frozen in

37

icebergs or running in deep underground pools. Of the total global fresh water supply, only about 3% is contained in the earth's lakes and rivers.

Fresh Water

A clear indication that fresh water is a finite resource is the fact that many areas of the world are beginning to experience periodic water shortages. The Middle East, Africa, parts of Central America, and the western United States have all had to cope with severe shortages of usable water in recent years. These shortages are not caused by a sudden or mysterious absence of water. The supply of safe, fresh water is threatened by growing populations, intense agricultural and industrial demands, and increasing amounts of pollution.

Humans often decrease the amount of usable water by contaminating it. Many lakes, rivers, and underground reservoirs are suffering from excess amounts of municipal *sewage,* industrial waste, and agricultural and urban runoff. These wastes damage both groundwater and surface water, often beyond repair.

Serious problems result when people cannot get enough clean water to drink and do not find ways to dispose of unclean water. The lack of clean water and proper sanitation poses the most serious economic and health threats in developing countries. The book *World Resources 1987* reports that approximately 80% of all human disease is associated with unsafe drinking water, poor sanitation, and ignorance about hygiene and how disease spreads. About one-quarter of the world's population—about 1.3 billion people—do not have access to safe drinking water. Another 1.5 billion people have no sanitary waste disposal facilities.

Each year, at least 25 million deaths in underdeveloped countries result from waterborne illnesses. Waterborne illnesses are caused by water contamination. Bacteria and viruses—microorganisms that often appear in water supplies as a result of overflow from sewers and septic tanks—can cause gastrointestinal diseases. These include trachoma blindness, affecting 500 million people worldwide, and elephantiasis, affecting 250 million people worldwide. These illnesses kill more than a thousand children every hour and contribute to widespread malnutrition. Cholera, typhoid, infectious hepatitis, poliomyelitis, and intestinal worms are other diseases that spread through contaminated water.

Disease-carrying human excrement is the most dangerous form of water pollution. In many less developed nations, lack of knowledge about hygiene, combined with social taboos, interferes with safe disposal of human wastes. Lack of adequate sanitation facilities, in turn, allows disease to spread easily. Efforts to educate people about hygiene helps to decrease the occurrence of water-related diseases.

Overuse and Industrial Pollution

According to *Water: Rethinking Management in an Age of Scarcity* by Sandra Postel of the Worldwatch Institute, world water use more than tripled between 1950 and 1980. On a worldwide scale, 73% of usable water is used for irrigation, 21% for industry, and 6% for domestic purposes. Unfortunately, most of the water designated for irrigating crops is used inefficiently: crops are often overwatered, so excess water is lost through evaporation when the ground no longer absorbs it.

In the United States, 50% of the fresh water supply is used to irrigate crops for feeding livestock. In comparison, approximately 35% of the fresh water is used to irrigate food crops that people eat directly. In California, where cattle sales constitute only one five-thousandth of the state's income, the largest amount of water goes to maintaining crops that only livestock will eat.

In industrialized countries, major sources of water pollution result from toxic industrial and mining operations. In the United States, the organic chemical and plastics industries produce the largest amounts of toxic chemical pollution. Other producers of toxic chemicals are pulp and paper industries, metal foundries, and petroleum refineries.

A March 27, 1989, article in *Time* magazine named five main contaminants found in water supplies. Although one of these involves bacteria and viruses, the other four contaminants result from human technology. For instance, chlorinated solvents, used for industrial purposes such as degreasing and chemical manufacturing, are thought to cause cancer. Trihalomethanes, which form as a chemical reaction

The children of New Mexico farmers play in an irrigation ditch near their home.

when water is purified by chlorine, can cause cancer and damage the liver and kidneys. Polychlorinated biphenyls, or PCBs, are the waste products that result from manufacturing systems, particularly out-moded ones, and from electric transformers. They can lead to liver damage and cancer. The toxic element *lead* often comes from old pipes and solder used in public water supplies and older private homes. Harmful effects of lead may include brain damage, high blood pressure, and nerve disorders.

Industrial waste, which is often hazardous, is seldom recycled or destroyed. Instead, in the United States two-thirds of hazardous waste is disposed of in wells or landfills, areas that allow easy contamination of groundwater. The United States has more than 77,000 sites that take in 82 billion gallons—the equivalent of 330 gallons for every man, woman, and child in the country—of hazardous waste each day. Typically, these sites are not designed to prevent seepage to the under-lying groundwater, and therefore they pose serious safety threats to our groundwater supplies.

Spills and Other Hazards

Chemical and oil spills are another type of contamination that causes damage that is difficult or impossible to repair. Unfortunately, such spills became increasingly common in the 1970s and 1980s. The EPA documented more than 7,000 accidents between 1980 and 1985 and in each of these years more than 20 of the incidents were major spills of more than 1 million gallons of oil or chemicals. Toxic pollutants also come from urban, mining, and agricultural areas where hazardous substances eventually get washed into the larger water supply through rainfall.

Agriculture also contributes to water pollution by introducing fertilizers, pesticides, herbicides, and animal wastes into freshwater supplies. The groundwater of 30 states in the United States has proven to be polluted by more than 60 pesticides, many of them carcinogens. In addition, water used to irrigate crops leaches salt from the soil before it runs off, carrying excess salt into rivers, lakes, and groundwater. Wastes from livestock constitute another large portion of agricultural

Wetlands help to filter and clean polluted water and to provide a habitat for many species of fish and birds, but they are rapidly disappearing as they are filled in to build housing developments.

pollution. Grazing animals produce five times as much waste as humans, and some animal wastes get into freshwater supplies. In addition to lakes and rivers, *wetlands* are another threatened water resource. Wetlands are moisture-saturated areas located where land and ocean meet. Oceans cover most of the earth and contain a vast variety of species. Yet more than half of the ocean's life forms dwell within 200 miles of shore, an area that also supplies most of the world's people

with seafood. The most abundant areas, situated along islands and coasts, are often referred to as wetlands.

Wetlands serve many essential functions. They are vital to replenishing groundwater because they act as a natural purifier. The tiny plants that live in water function as filters, absorbing excess nutrients and breaking down pesticides and other toxins. Despite their importance, wetlands are often threatened by overharvesting, construction and development, and pollution from industrial and municipal wastes. Half of the original wetlands in the continental United States have recently disappeared, at an annual loss of 450,000 acres, an area half the size of the state of Rhode Island, due to urban and agricultural development. As the wetlands shrink, they are less capable of processing ever-increasing amounts of pollution.

Four of the world's most productive ecosystems are wetlands. Situated in warm climates, coral reefs contain more plants and animal groups than any other ecosystem on earth and support one-third of all fish species. They also act as flood barriers to prevent erosion and storm damage. Yet reef systems require a delicate balance of clear water, bright sunlight, high salt levels, and water temperatures over

Offshore oil rigs and the accidental oil spills associated with them pollute the seas and threaten the existence of many marine creatures that humans depend on for food.

70°F. Unfortunately, these needs are easily disrupted by erosion, dumping, and dredging, any of which may cause the water to become cloudy and block essential sunlight.

Two other systems also thrive in warm climates—salt marshes and mangroves. Salt marshes are found in temperate zones, while mangroves are situated in tropical zones. In addition to filtering pollution, these systems support the growth of natural habitats for shellfish and other creatures by trapping nutrients and preventing erosion.

The fourth highly productive ecosystem is made up of estuaries, areas where fresh water washes silt into salty ocean water. These areas support a complex and complete food chain for creatures from protozoa to mammals. Yet estuaries tend to form in basins, a feature that enables pollution to collect. This buildup of pollution harms many life forms and adds contaminants to the human food supply.

Damage at Sea

More than half of the United States population lives within 50 miles of the sea. In fact, most of the world's people live near seacoasts or rivers that flow into seas. Despite their dependence on the sea, humans cause most of the damage that occurs in coastal regions. Human pollution harms a marine area's ability to provide food for sea animals and, in turn, humans. For instance, one-third of United States shellfish beds have already closed because of pollution. In addition, the United States is reporting growing numbers of cases of contaminated seafood, which can cause illnesses such as cholera, hepatitis, and gastroenteritis.

According to the book *Gaia: An Atlas of Planet Management* edited by Norman Myers, over 80% of all ocean pollution is caused by land-based activities. These originate from "point" and "nonpoint" sources. Point sources refer to pipes, ditches, and canals that contain sewage and industrial wastes. Nonpoint sources of ocean pollution include unregulated runoff from rain that carries agricultural, industrial, and urban contaminants to the sea. Urban runoff often combines with municipal sewage systems via storm sewers. Agricultural runoff carries fertilizers, pesticides, and herbicides and contains large amounts of nitrogen and phosphorous, substances that encourage the

SHAPING THE WATER: BLESSING OR BURDEN?

In recent years, technology has enabled humans to redesign or reroute water systems that nature took years to create. At first glance, these technological changes appear to greatly benefit humankind. But over the long term, these changes often cause irreparable damage to delicate ecosystems on which humans depend. Maintaining the fine balance in the natural environment is often necessary to sustain plant and animal life that also helps humans survive.

Water development projects, including dams, canals, and channels, may seriously upset water use and quality. They often increase the occurrence of waterborne diseases, destroy farmlands and wetlands, and interrupt delicately balanced habitats. For example, the building of large dams has recently been accompanied by an increase in waterborne diseases.

One of the most prevalent waterborne diseases is a debilitating illness called schistosomiasis. Caused by parasites that live in artificial reservoirs and irrigation systems, schistosomiasis does not kill its victims, but cripples them. Its spread is directlytincrease of artificial lakes, which are contaminated primarily by human feces. Although these lakes may at first seem to help people in their region, they eventually create health risks that no one had bargained for, particularly the engineers who designed them.

growth of algae. This rapidly reproducing plant depletes oxygen and sunlight, resources that other life forms depend on for survival. Certain algae also contain toxins that can directly harm plants and animals.

Despite legislation to limit ocean dumping, many nations continue to do so. The largest source of ocean dumping is dredging, clearing waterways for ships or for construction by digging up and removing soil from rivers, harbors, and channels. These unwanted materials are later dumped in another area of the ocean, often upsetting that area's natural balance.

Ocean dumping also involves municipal sewage, much of which is not treated before being dumped directly into the sea offshore. Often this washes back into harbors from the sea. Among other dumped wastes is sludge, or solid sewage residue. Currently, only two nations are known to dump sludge in the ocean—the United States and the United Kingdom. In fact, each year New York City and its neighboring communities dump over 8 million tons of sludge approximately 106 miles off the coast. In many cases, sludge may not be harmful; however, it can poison marine species if it contains PCBs, pesticides, toxic heavy metals, or disease-causing microorganisms. Sewage sludge also threatens marine life when it contains nutrients that encourage the growth of algae.

Technological industries also dump wastes into the ocean. Industrial, radioactive, and incinerated hazardous wastes all contain chemical pollutants that can reduce oxygen levels in sea water and thus threaten marine life. Oil pollution is yet another type of industrial waste that degrades ocean waters.

Each year approximately 3 to 6 million metric tons of oil are released into the oceans. Surprisingly, most of this oil waste is not a result of accidental spills. Spills from tankers account for less than one-third of all oil pollution. The main source of oil pollution at sea is the shipping industry. About one ton of oil is discharged for every thousand tons transported.

Humans also have more direct ways of permanently altering and damaging coastal areas. The influx of people living within 50 miles of the ocean leads to increased construction of homes and businesses. But this additional building often requires dredging and filling along

Even pristine mountain streams may one day no longer provide clean drinking water if the forests that filter the water are destroyed.

coastal areas. This, in turn, stirs up sediment that changes salt levels and water clarity, thus damaging delicate ecosystems. Sometimes the sediment may contain toxins, which cause further destruction. Unfortunately, the most thriving coastal areas are the calm, protected ones— the exact places preferred by humans for development. Ironically, as more humans strive to live closer to coastal regions where water is abundant, they create more stress on their water supply. As this trend continues, people are becoming increasingly aware that their environment has certain physical limitations.

CHAPTER 4

AIR: UNSEEN, UNCLEAN?

A lone tree, damaged by acid rain, stands against a deceptively picturesque sky that bathed it in nitric and sulfuric acids.

Taking in nutrients, using them for energy, and then releasing them in a different form, as wastes, is a normal part of the life process. All living creatures release wastes, but one species' wastes may be another species' nutrients. For example, animals breathe in oxygen and release carbon dioxide, while plants absorb carbon dioxide and release oxygen. Unfortunately, this balance is difficult to maintain when one species releases much more waste than another.

When humans release more carbon dioxide than their environment can handle, the entire atmosphere begins to suffer. The stress that humans are putting on the environment involves more than the carbon dioxide that people exhale. The human body itself does not generate as much waste as the machines that the human mind has created. Much unclean air comes from automobiles, energy-producing facilities, and industrial equipment.

Air pollution can damage the body either by short-term exposure at high levels or by long-term exposure at low levels. It can cause breathing difficulties; susceptibility to respiratory infections; chronic, or long-term, lung disease; worsening of heart and lung disease; fetal defects; and cancer. Emphysema, one of the most common respiratory disorders, is often attributed to atmospheric pollution or cigarette smoking. Its symptoms—including coughing, the frequent production of phlegm, and shortness of breath—gradually worsen over many years and may lead to heart strain. Infants, children, the elderly, and people with existing respiratory problems tend to show increased sensitivity to air pollution. Urban areas also add to this threat because they tend to have much higher levels of air pollutants.

Major Air Pollutants

The major pollutants harming the earth's atmosphere and human health are composed mainly of five substances—sulfur dioxide, nitrogen oxide, carbon monoxide, particulates, and airborne lead. In some cases, some of these harmful substances combine to form gases that cause further ill effects. Most of these substances are invisible to the naked eye, making them difficult to detect and easy to ignore. However, the body is very efficient at absorbing and processing gases and fine particles, which allows these substances easily to reach and harm various organs and body systems.

Sulfur dioxide is a corrosive gas that damages the human lungs and respiratory tract. It harms the environment by adding acid to water in soil, streams, and lakes. Its causes are attributed in equal parts to natural and human sources. Natural sources include volcanoes, decaying organic matter, and sea spray, while human sources include the burning of sulfur-containing coal and petroleum products and the smelting of nonferrous, or noniron, ore. The largest single source of sulfur dioxide is the human use of *fossil fuels* to generate electricity.

Nitrogen oxide causes the same health and environmental damage as sulfur dioxide. However, while rates of sulfur dioxide have decreased in the past two decades because of better controls on coal-burning power plants, nitrogen oxide levels have not improved owing to the ever-increasing use of automobile fuel. At least half of the nitrogen oxide released by humans comes from motor vehicles, while another third comes from power plants, and the rest comes from industrial production. Natural sources of nitrogen oxide are lightning and decomposing organic matter.

When carbon monoxide is inhaled, it restricts the body's ability to absorb oxygen, which in turn may cause impaired vision, poor coordination, and angina, a disease of the throat and chest marked by severe, suffocating pain. All of these symptoms reflect damage to the cardiovascular, pulmonary, and nervous systems. Most of the carbon monoxide emissions worldwide come from natural sources. But urban areas often show high levels of the gas, which comes from incomplete burning of fuels from motor vehicles.

Materials suspended in the air, either in solid or liquid form, are referred to as particulates. Smaller particulates can permeate the body and cause eye and lung damage. Although larger particulates reduce visibility in the atmosphere, they can be less harmful to health because they are too large to enter the body or interfere with its processes. Sources of particulates include dust, forest fires, and the burning of certain fuels. Fortunately, emissions controls are beginning to reduce the amount of particulates released by several industrial nations. Nevertheless, the United States Office of Technology Assessment estimates that particulates may contribute to the premature death of 50,000 Americans annually—almost 2% of the country's annual mortality rate.

Lead, if absorbed in large quantities, can harm the neurological, or nervous, system and cause kidney disease. Lead also damages plants

Trees draw carbon compounds from the air and store them in their tissues. When the forests are destroyed, the level of carbon dioxide in the atmosphere increases, threatening dramatic climate changes.

by interfering with respiration and photosynthesis, and prevents the decomposition of microorganisms. Additionally, after lead enters an ecosystem, the metal does not disappear. Today, the burning of leaded gasoline is the greatest source of lead pollution, followed by piping, roofing, and coin minting. Fortunately, strict emission standards have drastically reduced lead output since the 1970s.

Ozone Layer Depletion

While many substances are clearly dangerous, others may become health threats only in certain situations. Thus, they may mutate, or change, from harmless to harmful substances. A crucial example of this mutability is *ozone,* an invisible gas similar to oxygen. At ground level, ozone can be hazardous. But at greater heights it is an essential ingredient for protecting the earth's atmosphere. At heights between 10 and 30 miles above the earth's surface, ozone forms a layer of molecules that filter ultraviolet, or UV, radiation, energy released by the sun's powerful rays. Until recently this relatively thin layer of ozone surrounded the entire globe and protected its surface from hazardous UV rays. But recent reports show that a huge hole now exists in the ozone layer above the South Pole. Other ozone holes have been detected above the North Pole and in various other areas of the atmosphere.

Ultraviolet rays can harm individuals as well as the environment. In small amounts UV rays cause sunburn and rapid aging of skin, while long-term effects are linked to skin cancer and eye disorders, including retinal damage and cataracts. UV rays also decrease the immune system's ability to resist infection and disease.

Ultraviolet radiation also harms the plant kingdom in several ways. It decreases photosynthesis, which results in stunted leaf growth, damaged seed quality, and, in turn, reduced crop yields. UV radiation also destroys many of the smaller plant and animal species at the bottom of ecosystem food chains. Starvation can then occur among larger animals that depend on the smaller organisms for food.

One of the major causes of ozone depletion is the use of chlorofluorocarbons, or CFCs, chlorine-based by-products of an artificial compound invented in the 1930s for use in refrigerants, coolants, solvents, foam-blowing agents, and aerosol propellants. For years the compound was hailed as a miracle—an all-purpose chemical with no negative side effects. However, when researchers discovered and began to investigate the ozone hole, they found that many CFCs had collected in the stratosphere and were causing extensive damage to the ozone layer. CFCs have been estimated to cause about 20% of the ozone layer's demise. When CFCs interact with UV radiation in the stratosphere, they break down into chlorine atoms. A single one of these atoms can destroy 100,000 ozone molecules, offsetting the balance of oxygen and ozone in this fragile layer.

This ozone plot of the southern hemisphere, made by the National Aeronautics and Space Administration, reveals that more and more ultraviolet radiation is reaching the earth's surface as a result of ozone depletion.

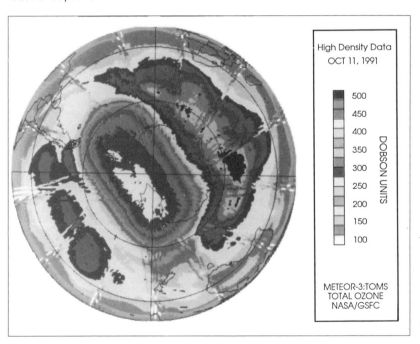

As early as the 1970s, the American researchers Sherwood Rowland and Mario Molina warned that the upper layers of the earth's atmosphere were suffering damage from CFCs. Although these findings were ignored at first, by 1986 the world's leading industrial nations signed the Montreal Protocol, a plan put forth by the United Nations Environment Program, to stop the use of ozone-depleting chemicals by the year 2000. More than 30 countries are now involved in the plan, a worldwide recognition that all nations must work together to protect the environment and public health.

But damage to the ozone layer affects much more than the earth's stratosphere. As this layer thins and more of the sun's rays enter the atmosphere, the earth may gradually begin to grow warmer. This long-term warming of the planet may have been set in motion by recent chemical changes in the atmosphere.

The Greenhouse Effect

The overproduction of certain gases may be causing a change in the composition of the earth's atmosphere, an alteration referred to as *global warming*. Scientists became concerned when they discovered the role of certain gases in accelerating the *greenhouse effect*. The earth's outer atmosphere, they say, acts like the glass that encloses a greenhouse, which allows the sun's rays to enter as visible light but does not allow heat to escape.

After the sun's visible light hits the earth's surface, it radiates off the surface as invisible heat rays, called infrared rays. In the past, much of the infrared radiation could escape through the atmosphere back into outer space. Today, however, the accumulation of excess gases and chemicals released by humans over the past hundred years has created a layer of pollution that prevents some infrared rays from escaping the earth's atmosphere. These formations of chemicals and gases appear to have caused small but noticeable changes in the climate, with a particular tendency toward warming.

While temperatures at the earth's surface have risen approximately 1°F over the past century, some scientists expect them to rise more

Environmental activists in Cleveland, Ohio, protest industrial air pollution.

dramatically in the next century as levels of carbon dioxide continue to increase. Although a 1°F change may sound insignificant, one must consider that such a change usually takes thousands of years to occur naturally. Over dozens of centuries, plant and animal species are normally able to adapt to very gradual trends in warming. However,

today's changes are happening so fast that many species may not be capable of adapting quickly enough.

In theory, rising global temperatures can cause several changes. For one, changes in weather may become extreme in certain regions. Some areas may become much warmer and drier than they are now, while others become much cooler and wetter. Some areas could suffer from extremes of hot summers and cold winters, while others would grow generally warmer with a dramatic increase in the number of warm days in winter and hot days in summer. Warmer winters would result in lower levels of snowfall, causing soil in these areas to be drier and less productive. The possibility of this trend causes some scientists to speculate that America's great midwestern plains may become deserts, while Canada's cold northern states might then become the continent's "bread basket."

If global warming continues to be a real threat, sea levels will also rise. Higher atmospheric temperatures could cause the polar ice caps to melt and this long-frozen water would then spread outward and raise sea levels around the world. Also, ocean water would expand when heated, further raising sea levels and resulting in flooded coastal areas. Eventually, people would need to move further inland to avoid floods. This trend is apparently already beginning to occur along the north-eastern United States coast, where the sea level has risen approximately one foot in the past 100 years. In fact, the EPA predicts it may rise another seven feet by the year 2100.

The possibility of global warming poses other threats as well. Many species which have adapted to their environments over thousands of years may not be able to survive a sudden increase in temperature, even by just a few degrees. For instance, many trees cannot tolerate overall temperature changes greater than 2°F. Tree species can migrate over a 125-mile range in the direction of a cooler climate, but this type of change requires at least a century to occur—a rate that may not keep up with global warming.

The difficulty that other life forms have adapting to climate change would also affect humans. In response to permanent weather changes, crops would need expensive technologies to survive in areas that had grown hotter and drier than their original environment. Meanwhile, as food crops struggled harder to adapt, hardier plants, such as weeds, would thrive under these circumstances and threaten food crops. This phenomenon also would apply to insects, which thrive in warmer climates and have short life spans, making it easy for them to evolve rapidly. These types of parasites would attack and eat increasingly weakened agricultural crops.

Greenhouse Gases and Acid Rain

The excess gases that appear to be contributing to the greenhouse effect are usually referred to as greenhouse gases. The most threatening greenhouse gas, thought to be responsible for 50% of the greenhouse effect, is carbon dioxide. It is the by-product released in the largest quantities during the burning of fossil fuels to create energy. Deforestation also increases carbon dioxide levels when acres of trees and plants are burned or left to rot.

Hydrocarbons, also referred to as volatile organic compounds, are another type of greenhouse gas. Incomplete burning of fossil fuels through motor vehicle exhaust is their major human source. Sources from nature include fires and the decomposition of once-living matter. Hydrocarbons are suspected of causing cancer, mutations, and birth defects. These gases are especially hazardous because, when near the earth's surface, sunlight causes them to mix with other compounds and produce new pollutants, such as low-level ozone, another greenhouse gas.

Low-level ozone is formed near ground level when sunlight causes chemical interactions between nitrogen oxides and organic compounds. These interactions can lead to serious air pollution. In the United States, low-level ozone is especially harmful to those 16 million Americans with emphysema, asthma, and other respiratory ailments. Low-level ozone may also contribute to eye irritation, nasal congestion, reduced lung functioning, and even damaged lung tissue. Low-level ozone is also an important component of smog. Smog is a common air pollutant in urban areas, especially in summer when the sun causes it to interact strongly with other pollutants to form a new blend of even more dangerous chemicals. Another greenhouse gas, methane, comes from rice paddies, swamps, cattle and livestock, termites, wood burning, and landfills. Sulfur and nitrogen oxides are also included among the greenhouse gases.

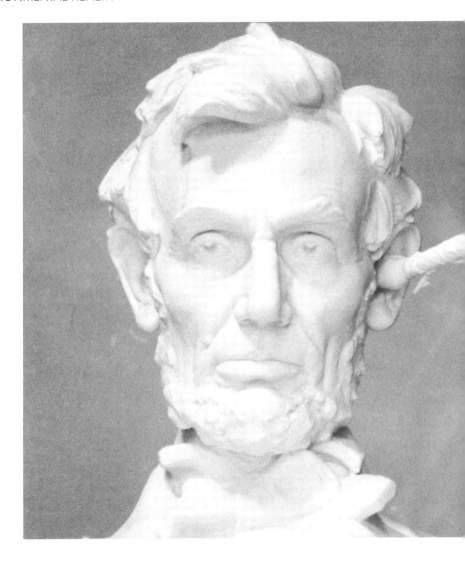

As scientists see the increasing threat of the greenhouse effect and other results of air pollution, they search for ways to remedy these problems. Experts are working to improve energy efficiency, control the use of fossil fuels, and limit the use of harmful gases and chemicals. They continue searching for ways to reverse deforestation and to increase the use of renewable energy sources, such as solar and wind power.

Acids and other pollutants in the atmosphere can damage stone monuments. Here a National Parks Service employee cleans the statue of Abraham Lincoln at the Lincoln Memorial in Washington, D.C.

As the air becomes more polluted, it begins to contaminate other elements it contacts, such as water. One of the most damaging and controversial forms of air pollution in the world may be *acid deposition,* the official name given to what many people call acid rain. Acid deposition begins with emissions of gases such as sulfur oxide from coal-burning electric power plants and nitrogen oxide from motor vehicles. Once these substances enter the atmosphere, they become tiny particles that attach to moisture, which then becomes part of clouds, fog, rain, sleet, snow, or dry particles. Often this moisture is held in clouds in the upper atmosphere, then travels to regions far removed from its source before it falls as precipitation.

When acidic water falls, it kills organisms or inhibits their ability to reproduce. Even if only a few species are harmed, all the other living organisms in the ecosystem will suffer as a result. In addition, acidic water falls in reservoirs that contain water for human consumption. The acidic water leaches metals from pipes, adding metal to drinking water. The acidic fallout also damages buildings, many of which are historic monuments. For example, the famous Parthenon in Athens and other ancient Greek temples have suffered significant acid rain damage in the past 20 years. Finally, scientists are reporting that trees are dying at a rapid rate because acid rain is leaching nutrients, such as calcium, magnesium, and potassium, from leaves and soil. In some cases the acid harms leaves and roots so that they are no longer able to carry nutrients to the tree. The acid also releases aluminum from the soil, causing tree roots to rot. Similarly, the aluminum enters streams and lakes, another threat to public water supplies.

Acid rain is doubly dangerous when it combines with ozone at ground level, a combination that can destroy both plants and forests. This is suspected to be the main cause of forests declining in the United States, Canada, and Europe. Large sections of Germany's historic Black Forest, for instance, have been severely affected by this lethal combination. At higher elevations, damage may be two or three times worse than it is lower down the mountainside because pollutants are more concentrated at higher elevations. Although this damage has been known to occur in highly industrial areas, it now seems to be spreading to forests far removed from cities.

Perhaps the most dangerous aspect of air pollution is its invisibility. Because people cannot see the pollution, they often do not recognize its dangers. Yet gases spread through the atmosphere much more easily than other substances. They also spread easily through the human body, sometimes creating long-term, irreparable harm. To avoid this harm, people must recognize and do something about the very real threat of breathing unclean air.

CHAPTER 5

WORK: AN INVISIBLE KILLER?

Many workers confront hazardous conditions every day on their jobs. Stress as well as physical injury is a serious risk.

Americans are more likely to die from work-related disease and injury than from any other preventable cause," reports the National Workplace Institute, an independent research group in Chicago. Based on a study of mortality data, the Institute concludes that in 1987, 71,000 Americans died of cancer and cardiovascular and neurological problems related to their working conditions. The Institute called occupational disease "America's invisible killer . . . the most neglected public health problem in the United States today.

The National Institute of Occupational Safety and Health, or NIOSH, has sampled 5,000 workplaces and found that they contain 8,000 potentially toxic substances. Yet the Occupational Safety and Health Administration, or OSHA, the branch of the U.S. Department of Labor that collects and analyzes chemical samples from workplaces, regulates the use of only about 500 of these substances. In fact, at present the true number of threatening substances in the workplace and their effects on the human body can only be speculated.

Symptoms of occupational illness may include headaches, nose and throat irritation, blurred vision, dizziness, blackout spells, disorientation, and coughing up blood. Symptoms that tend to disappear in the evenings and on weekends, but reappear on Monday morning, may be related to working conditions. The most severe cases, caused by ongoing exposure to toxins, may lead to cancer and death.

Industrial Work Hazards

While people have long feared cancer in the workplace, recent concern has grown over the effects of certain chemicals on organs and organ systems, particularly the nervous system. The nervous system includes the brain, spinal cord, and nerves, which help the brain and body communicate. Bodily contamination that harms the nervous system is often referred to as neurotoxicity.

"Chronic neurotoxicity presents a health risk every bit as large and as tragic as cancer, yet almost nothing is being done about it. Our regulatory system is virtually blind to the risk," claimed Albert Gore, Jr., in 1990 when he was chairman of the Subcommittee on Science, Technology, and Space. At that time, the committee released a federal study on neurotoxicity stating that 65,000 toxic substances and chemicals were currently in use. Many of these toxins can damage the nervous system, contributing to Parkinson's disease, Alzheimer's disease, and Lou Gehrig's disease. The most common neurotoxic chemicals are found in industrial chemicals and drugs, food additives, and cosmetics.

The petrochemical industry has been under frequent attack for showing lack of concern for worker safety. According to the National Workplace Institute, the rate of fatal accidents in the petrochemical industry has doubled within the past decade. While fatalities averaged 10 deaths a year from 1971 through the early 1980s, the death rate doubled from 1987 into the early 1990s due to an outbreak of accidents at refineries and chemical plants. Experts speculate that increased accidents may be tied to the downturn in the economy. Some petrochemical plants tried to increase production while using fewer full-time workers, thus increasing risks of on-the-job accidents. More than 40,000 jobs in the refinery industry and 30,000 in the chemical industry have been cut since 1982.

According to NIOSH, lung diseases are the most common ailment among industrial workers. Diseases that are caused by the accumulation of dust in the lungs, which, in turn, causes a severe reaction in the lung tissue, are generally referred to as pneumoconioses. These diseases, which originate from different types of particles and dust, include asbestosis, byssinosis, silicosis, and coal worker's pneumoconiosis. Other lung diseases that can be work-related are asthma and lung cancer.

Asbestosis is caused by *asbestos,* a mineral-based, noncombustible building material. Construction workers, automobile maintenance workers, and shipbuilders all work with asbestos on a regular basis. Byssinosis frequently occurs among textile workers who are exposed to cotton dust, and even appears in retired textile workers who no longer encounter the substance on a regular basis. Workers exposed to silica in mines, foundries, and stone and glass industries may be afflicted with silicosis. Coal worker's pneumoconiosis, also called "black lung," develops from repeated exposure to coal dust.

Although tobacco smoke is considered the most frequent cause of lung cancer, many work-related substances are also associated with the disease. Common workplace carcinogens include arsenic, asbestos, chromates, ionizing radiation, metal particles, and polynuclear aromatic hydrocarbons, or PAHs, hazardous types of chemical pollutants.

In Long Beach, California, asbestos workers protest their company's unwillingness to provide adequate health protection for those exposed to this carcinogen.

Many of these agents become much more dangerous when combined with tobacco smoke.

Lung cancer is not the only form of cancer that occurs frequently among people who work around these chemicals. For example, bladder cancer has high rates among dye workers. Pancreatic and rectal cancer occurs more frequently among thorium refinery workers, and high leukemia rates coincide with workers who use benzene-based compounds when manufacturing shoes, rubber tires, or glue.

Office Hazards

Although industrial occupations seem to pose the greatest threat, even office workers encounter unhealthy conditions on a continual basis.

The National Workplace Institute study claims that the recent increase in the number and kinds of service occupations has brought new workplace illnesses caused by stress, indoor air pollution, and new, untested chemical compounds.

According to an EPA report released in May 1989, indoor air quality is among America's top environmental health problems. The report stated that a major portion of air pollution is received indoors and may result in acute and chronic health threats. The term acute refers to sudden, short-term symptoms, while the term chronic refers to an ongoing condition. Potential ill effects range from itchy eyes and runny noses to permanent organ damage and even death from lung cancer and other diseases. Of course, these effects depend on the amount of exposure to toxins and on each individual's susceptibility.

Major sources of indoor air pollution include environmental to-bacco smoke, building materials, furnishings, and office equipment. These materials release fumes containing volatile organic compounds, including *formaldehyde* (an irritant) and polynuclear aromatic hydro-carbons, as well as asbestos and many other toxins. Any of these substances, most of which are carcinogens, can contaminate indoor air. Discomfort that is attributed to ongoing unhealthy conditions in a building is called Sick Building Syndrome. In the early 1990s, a World Health Organization committee estimated that 30% of new or recently remodeled buildings receive high numbers of complaints of building-related illnesses.

The two most obvious barriers to clean indoor air are poor ventila-tion and a lack of access to fresh air. Many offices are designed to allow executives and managers private office space with windows that can open to fresh outdoor air. Meanwhile, their support staff may be crowded into cubicles in a central space, often with inadequate venti-lation and lighting. Crowded office spaces become stuffy and accumu-late carbon monoxide and carbon dioxide, making workers feel tired and depressed.

Modern buildings are tightly sealed to help conserve energy and they depend on ventilation systems to recycle their air supply. Yet many unsafe substances can and often do enter and flow throughout the ventilation system indefinitely. These substances are given off by paint, which often contains lead; insulation materials, which contain asbestos; carpets and furnishings, which frequently contain formaldehyde; and photocopy machines and laser printers, which produce low-level ozone. These materials release fumes and gases that may become trapped in the ventilation systems of airtight buildings. Bacteria and fungi also enter ventilation systems and then circulate through ducts into every office in the building. An improperly cleaned and maintained ventilation system is even more likely to spread these contaminants. Similarly, tobacco smoke can circulate from one worker who smokes to many workers who do not. With no place to go, many people are forced to breathe these substances on a continual basis.

Radiation and Lighting

Electrical equipment used in offices and other public buildings may pose a newly discovered threat of radioactivity. This form of potentially harmful radiation originates from an *electromagnetic field.* Many everyday objects that use energy involve a combination of electric and magnetic fields, including power lines, computers, lamps, and even beepers.

Because power lines produce extremely high-voltage electric and magnetic fields, they have become the focus of studies on possible effects of electromagnetic fields. According to the book *Radiation Alert* by David I. Puch, one study revealed that 450,000 Canadian male workers who were frequently exposed to the high-voltage fields around power lines were three times more likely to die of leukemia, a deadly form of cancer, than those workers who were not exposed.

Video display terminals, or VDTs, the screens used with every computer, are also a controversial subject in reference to possible health risks. Many people who use computers and VDT screens regularly complain about eyestrain, neck soreness, and headaches. Due to the electromagnetic radiation they release, VDTs have recently been linked to miscarriages in women who use computers extensively. A study conducted by the Kaiser-Permanente medical program in Oakland, California, found that working pregnant women who used VDTs

Continuously exposed to hazardous waste, these employees of the Environmental Protection Agency must wear elaborate protective clothing and self-contained breathing apparatus.

for more than 20 hours a week tended to have 80% higher miscarriage rates than women who performed similar jobs without using VDTs.

VDTs also release light in pulses that appear so quickly that they are invisible, yet may lead to eyestrain and eye damage. Electromagnetic radiation remains a controversial topic. Various experts insist that no conclusive evidence of damage exists. But, for the cautious, one way to prevent these effects is to avoid looking directly at the computer screen when entering computer data and to use printouts for reading data files.

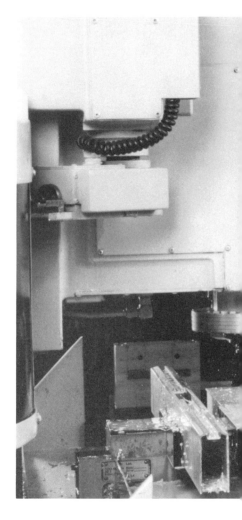

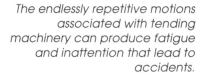

The endlessly repetitive motions associated with tending machinery can produce fatigue and inattention that lead to accidents.

Lighting is another area of office health that has just begun to gain attention as a possible health threat. Fluorescent lighting, which has been used for years in most offices and public places, is now recognized as unhealthy. Fluorescent light tubes do not include the full spectrum of light found in natural sunlight, and this lack of certain light rays can cause mood swings, depression, and decreased productivity. Similar to VDTs, fluorescent lights work by releasing small pulses of electric energy, which occur so rapidly that they seem continuous. Yet the pulses actually create constant flashes that lead to eyestrain, fatigue, and even central nervous system damage.

Noise Pollution

Noise is defined as unwanted sound. Of course, not every sound is unwanted, but when it becomes too loud it can cause serious damage. Sound is a wave moving through the air. The wave creates vibrations that hit the eardrum, which sends messages to the brain. Although sound does not accumulate in the air like other forms of pollution, it can create much damage in the short time that it touches the eardrum, depending on the level of the sound.

Loss of hearing is often caused by continued exposure to volumes of sound of 80–85 decibels. (A decibel is a unit that measures sound intensity.) Approximately 8 million United States production workers are exposed to these noise levels, and 1.5 million show measurable hearing loss as a result. Recent amplification systems for rock music have been measured at 125 decibels, a level which definitely contributes to hearing loss. Indeed, levels of 135 decibels can cause instant damage to hearing, while levels above 150 decibels can rupture the eardrum, causing permanent hearing loss. Continued noise over long periods of time also contributes to hearing loss. For example, people in large cities tend to lose their hearing as they grow older, whereas older people who have lived in quiet communities throughout their lives often hear as well as young people.

In addition to hearing loss, noise affects the nervous system by increasing anxiety and stress. In fact, loud or unexpected noises may even provoke a fright reaction. This sort of response causes the body to have increased heart rate and blood pressure, constricted blood vessels, digestive spasms, and dilation, or contraction, of the pupils. Research with animals indicates that long-term effects of noise pollution lead to heart, brain, and liver damage, as well as emotional stress. Furthermore, psychologists report that work efficiency in people decreases as noise levels rise.

Exposure to unhealthy conditions at work can be especially hazardous because workers face direct, concentrated, and continuous contact with the threat. Yet many workers are not aware of potential dangers. Many workplace warnings of health hazards tend to use overly technical and confusing language. Often, even the managers may not be fully aware of the threats of toxic materials or other dangers in the workplace. In addition, employees may hesitate to complain because they fear they may lose their jobs. And when employees do complain, many health care professionals have not been trained to recognize work-related illnesses, a lack of knowledge that may lead to incorrect identification of long-term illnesses. As more people learn about the possible risks found in work environments, much may be done to improve current working conditions.

CHAPTER 6

NO PLACE
LIKE HOME

Many common household medicines and prescription drugs can be dangerous if not taken in the proper dosages. These bottles have all been labeled with stickers featuring the phone numbers of local poison control centers.

There's no place like home" is a saying that shows how people view their homes: comfortable and safe. Yet homes are not always as safe as people like to believe, and they can be as dangerous as many other places. In fact, the threats found in a house or neighborhood can be especially dangerous because they are often unseen and unsuspected.

Building materials, furnishings, and cleaning products often contain substances that pose a threat to health. Many materials once used in building older homes have since been found to contain harmful substances. New homes often contain building materials that have not yet been tested for potentially hazardous ingredients. And while cleanliness is a virtue, cleaning materials can be dangerous if used or mixed improperly.

Many people think that no matter how dirty the outside air gets, they can escape into the safety of a clean home. Yet indoor air pollution can be worse than that found outdoors. Often, newly built homes are tightly sealed, which allows a buildup of colorless and odorless indoor contaminants. Indoor pollutants are generally categorized as either "detectable" or "undetectable" contaminants, based on whether or not their presence is easy or even possible to recognize without special testing.

Detectable Contaminants

Detectable contaminants may be recognized in a variety of ways. In addition to sight and smell, symptoms such as choking, burning eyes, difficult breathing, or asphyxiation can lead to instant detection. Common detectable contaminants include smoke from wood, coal, or kerosene fires, unvented stoves and ovens, gas and oil furnaces, and water heaters. Many detectable contaminants are present in household products, especially cleansers and disinfectants.

Tobacco smoke is among the most dangerous detectable indoor air pollutants. In 1989, the U.S. Surgeon General estimated that 400,000 Americans die from breathing their own tobacco smoke. But while many smokers recognize the risk they run, many people have no idea of the negative effects of secondhand smoke. Secondhand, or passive, smoke ranks behind firsthand smoke and alcohol as the third leading preventable cause of death in the United States.

At an international conference on lung disease in May 1990 in Boston, Dr. Stanton A. Glantz of the University of California at San Francisco reported that *passive smoke* kills approximately 50,000 Americans each year—two-thirds of whom die of heart disease. He found a 30% increase in risk of death from heart attacks among nonsmokers living with smokers, a risk that increases with heavier smokers.

Other findings also suggest that heart disease results from passive smoke. Dr. William B. Moskowitz at the Medical College of Virginia in Richmond reports that adolescent children whose parents smoke have a greater risk of heart disease. Young people who were exposed to tobacco smoke since birth showed higher levels of cholesterol and lower levels of HDL, a protein in blood that is believed to help prevent heart attacks. Again, the higher the exposure to smoke, the greater the risk of potential heart problems.

According to the EPA, tobacco smoke contains more than 4,700 compounds, including 43 carcinogens. A burning cigarette creates mainstream smoke, taken in when the smoker inhales, and sidestream smoke, released from the burning ends of cigarettes, pipes, and cigars. Mainstream smoke is composed of large particles that become lodged in the larger airways of the lungs, but sidestream smoke is composed of small particles that reach deeper into the lungs. Because of the incomplete burning of sidestream smoke, its mixture of gases and carcinogenic tar is dirtier. Mainstream smoke has been linked to cancers of the mouth, throat, larynx, esophagus, urinary bladder, kidney, and pancreas. Sidestream smoke has been linked to cancers of the brain, thyroid, and breast.

The American Academy of Pediatrics estimates that between 9 and 12 million American children under age five may be exposed to passive smoke. Since 1986, 30 reports have linked passive smoking with respiratory disorders, and researchers fear that passive smoking greatly increases the risk of early childhood respiratory illnesses, particularly bronchitis and pneumonia. According to the EPA, passive smoke may be especially harmful to an infant's immune and respiratory systems. Asthmatic children are at high risk, particularly because lung problems that develop in childhood often extend into adulthood.

Household Products

Many types of cleansers and disinfectants sold from store shelves daily can severely hurt anyone who uses them. Their threat varies, depending

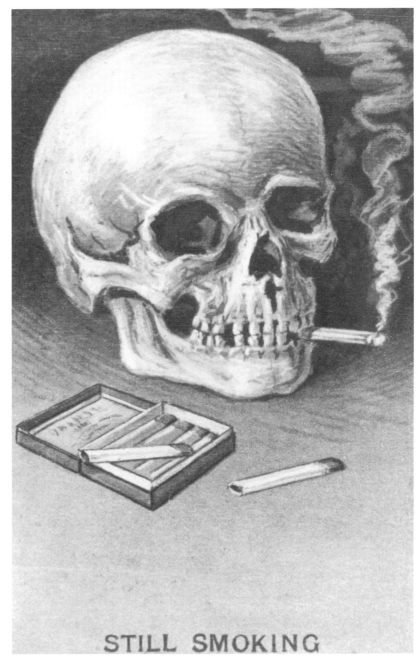

STILL SMOKING

An antismoking lithograph from 1910.

on which chemical is contained in each product. The list of household cleaners that could threaten human health is extremely long. Among the main offenders are aerosol vapors, air fresheners, insect sprays, and ammonia- or chlorine-containing cleaners.

All-purpose cleaners often contain chemicals such as ammonia, which can damage lungs, and chlorine, which creates cancer-causing compounds. Even worse, when ammonia and chlorine are combined, they form a deadly chloramine gas. For example, bleach is particularly harmful if mixed with ammonia because bleach contains chlorine, detergents, and synthetic dyes. Similar substances are present in laundry by-products. Disinfectants also contain toxic chemicals such as ammonia, chlorine, and phenol, which are so strong that they may even leak fumes through their containers.

Drain cleaners can be especially harmful because they contain hydrochloric and sulfuric acids, substances that can burn human tissue, and lye, a powerful caustic that can burn or disfigure human tissue. Lye, which is also found in oven cleaners, can cause blindness if splashed in the eyes. Anything containing lye should be kept away from children. Toilet cleaners can burn the skin and eyes due to highly toxic ingredients, such as chlorine and hydrochloric acid. Swallowing these substances could cause serious illness or death.

Automatic dishwashing powders contain strong agents with high levels of phosphates, substances released into rinse water that eventually reaches lakes and streams and kills fish and aquatic life. Dishwashing liquids, often made from nonbiodegradable petroleum products, frequently contain harmful dyes and fragrances. Even dyes and fragrances found in toilet paper can cause skin irritation and damage water systems.

For the past few decades, aerosols have been recognized as a cause of ozone destruction, yet their use has not been totally eliminated. In an effort to decrease levels of CFCs, the ozone-damaging substances used to propel ingredients out of aerosol cans, product manufacturers searched for ozone-safe substitutes. CFC propellants were replaced with butane, isobutane, and propane, new types of chemical propellants. Yet laboratory experiments indicate that these chemicals harm the heart and central nervous system in animals. As a result, experts

recommend that people stop using products packaged in aerosol cans and start using pump dispensers instead. Aerosol cans can also explode when pressurized or exposed to heat.

Batteries are another common household product that contain hazardous materials. Ingredients such as nickel, cadmium, and mercury can seriously harm people, animals, and fish. Because these

A crab stand at Fisherman's Wharf in San Francisco, California. In recent years, because of ocean pollution, the consumption of seafood has come to pose new risks for consumers.

materials are so toxic, batteries should be taken to their retailer for disposal, and mercury-containing batteries should be taken to a hazardous waste disposal center. Furthermore, if batteries are exposed to fire, they will explode.

Pesticides constitute another serious chemical hazard. The term *pesticide* is used to describe a variety of products that will kill unwanted animal pests and intruders, including insecticides, herbicides, fungicides, and rodenticides. All of these products are highly toxic, yet they are used in 90% of American homes. Pesticides are hazardous both during application and afterward, when residents unknowingly continue to inhale residues. In addition, furnishings such as carpets contain pesticides for mothproofing. Often pesticides are used in enclosed spaces, a practice that increases their threat.

Some Safe Alternatives

More and more people are becoming convinced that grandmother's old-fashioned recipes and remedies may have been wiser than they once realized. Despite the convenience of many newfangled inventions, many modern cleaning products are proving to be hazardous. Meanwhile the old tried and true formulas still work as well as they always have without toxic side effects, high prices, and wasteful packaging.

Common items found in the food pantry often can be used for more than one purpose. Baking soda is an all-purpose cleanser that removes odors, cleans teeth, acts as an antacid, and polishes just about everything. Thus, it is safe to ingest and is nonabrasive to surfaces. White vinegar cuts grease, prevents mold, and removes odors, and lemon juice also works as an excellent cleaner and grease cutter.

Mineral oil, sold at any pharmacy, works as a wood cleaner, furniture polish, and cleanser for greasy hands. Borax, found in the grocery store laundry section, can clean, remove odors, and prevent mold. However, it should not be swallowed and should be kept away from children.

Many people may not know that safer alternatives also exist to prevent unwanted pests. Beetles and weevils will stay away from flour and grain products containing a bay leaf. Ants will avoid indoor areas sprinkled with red chili powder, borax, or dried peppermint, and outside doorways where mint is planted. Cockroaches can be killed by sprinkling a nontoxic combination of equal parts baking soda and powdered sugar. Boric acid will also control roaches, but this powder should not be used near children or pets. Pyrethrin is an all-purpose bug-killer that remains safe if it is not combined with toxic pesticides.

Many pests can be avoided by preventing their appearance in the first place. Flies and mosquitoes can be eliminated by using screens on all windows. Hanging cloves or placing citrus peels in strategic locations will also keep flies away, while burning citronella oil, or growing garlic, marigolds, or any flowers that attract birds, will reduce mosquitoes. Feeding pets brewer's yeast, a powder that contains vitamin B, will make them immune to fleas. Fleas also can be prevented by using an organic spray containing eucalyptus, cedar wood, or bay leaves. Rats and mice are easily deterred by cats.

Undetectable Contaminants

Undetectable contaminants are especially threatening because they can affect people year after year without being discovered. Even when these substances appear in small quantities, over long periods of time their constant presence in enclosed spaces causes great harm. Their long-term effects involve damage to the central nervous system, lungs, heart, kidneys, and liver. These problems lead to symptoms such as dizziness, headaches, fatigue, and, in extreme cases, cancer.

Many undetectable contaminants are found in building materials, finishes, and furnishings. Asbestos was frequently used as a building material in houses built before the mid-1970s. It was extremely popular because it is durable and resists burning—useful qualities for insulating heating pipes, boilers, and panels placed behind wood stoves. Despite its benefits, however, asbestos is particularly dangerous because it is composed of invisible fibers that are so small that when released they float in the air and are easily inhaled. Once in the lungs, asbestos remains there and can lead to irreversible damage. As mentioned earlier, asbestos is linked to severe lung diseases, including asbestosis, mesothelioma, and lung cancer.

Although the EPA prohibits the further manufacture and use of asbestos, the material is already built into many buildings, including schools where many children may be exposed. In cases where asbestos

is already present, experts advise leaving it alone. However, if asbestos has begun to crumble or become powdery, one of three actions should be taken: removal, enclosure, or encapsulation. Removal is extremely difficult and must meet strict government regulations for safety, costing over $100 per hour to remove and risking the health of asbestos workers. Enclosure involves permanently covering up or closing off areas that contain asbestos. Encapsulation involves sealing asbestos-

The modern farmer often mixes chemical food additives and antibiotics into animal feed. These substances are then consumed by people. Not all the long-term effects of such chemicals are understood by scientists.

containing objects with paint, epoxy, or fiberglass cloth, particularly if they are too awkward to enclose.

Another undetectable contaminant used widely in building materials and household products is formaldehyde. This substance is contained in many glues, paints, and surface coatings. It is also used as a permanent press product in clothing and drapes. Formaldehyde is an irritant that causes symptoms such as burning eyes and throat, difficult breathing, nausea, and dermatitis, an irritating skin condition. It has been found to cause cancer in animals, suggesting that it may affect humans in the same way.

Indoors, formaldehyde is most commonly found in particleboard used in shelves, cabinets, furniture, and flooring, in wood paneling and fiberboard used for furniture tops and cabinet fronts, and in furnishings such as carpets, rugs, and upholstery. In the 1970s formaldehyde was used as foam insulation in a half million homes and mobile homes where it continues to release a gas, particularly in humid or exposed areas. Levels of formaldehyde in the home can be reduced by increasing room ventilation and using air conditioners or dehumidifiers to reduce humidity and warm temperatures. But the best way to avoid formaldehyde contamination is to avoid placing objects that contain it in the home.

Lead contamination has a variety of sources. It is a by-product of industrial smelting, battery manufacturing, and automobile engines. Lead from car exhaust that accumulates in city streets is particularly harmful to children who often play in these polluted areas. Fortunately, the presence of lead in gasoline has been reduced through EPA regulations over the past 10 years.

While levels of lead in gasoline are decreasing, the overall use of lead is increasing, particularly in indoor paint and in tin cans. Lead poisoning tends to concentrate in blood, bone, and soft tissue, which affects the nervous system, kidneys, and other organs. The danger is worsened because lead is not naturally excreted from the body.

Since the discovery of radon in 1984, public concern has grown about this new undetectable contaminant. Radon is a naturally occurring gas that cannot be seen, smelled, or tasted. It comes from the ground where the uranium in soil and rocks decays, a process that creates radiation. This form of radiation then seeps into homes through the cracks in their foundations or the water pipes in wells located in radon-laden areas. Once radon enters a home its radioactive particles can lodge in a person's lungs and cause cancer, a risk that increases for cigarette smokers.

Radon exists almost everywhere, but is not harmful when it decays in open air. However, as it accumulates in a confined space, such as a tightly insulated building, radon concentrations reach dangerous levels. Older, wooden homes which are not well insulated actually present less threat from radon, while tightly sealed brick or concrete homes tend to contain radon in more concentrated amounts.

Exposure to radon is measured in picocuries per liter of air or water, or pCi/L. A picocurie is one trillionth of a curie, which is a unit of radioactivity equalling one gram of radium. An annual level of 100 pCi/L creates as much radioactive exposure as having 2,000 chest X rays per year. According to EPA reports, radon exposure at this level would result in approximately 35 deaths in a community of 100 people. Exposure to just 2 pCi/L, the equivalent of 100 chest X rays per year, would lead to the death of one person in a community of 100 people. *Radon: The Citizen's Guide,* published by the Environmental Defense Fund, states that as many as 10 million households in North America are seriously threatened by radon exposure.

Radon levels can be measured through relatively simple tests. Although some tests can be purchased at local stores, these are not as accurate as those conducted by professionals who use up-to-date testing techniques. Once high levels of radon are detected in a home, they can be corrected, usually at a cost ranging between $500 and $2,000. People who want additional information about radon contamination can call 1-800-SOS-RADON.

Everyday Sources of Radiation

In addition to naturally occurring radiation, there are many man-made sources of ionizing, or highly active, radiation. Nuclear power plants, reactors, and toxic waste dumps pose an obvious threat of exposure to radiation, but these are not the only sources. Dangerous radiation can come from a variety of sources that people encounter every day, including many household and office devices, such as smoke detectors, ceramic tableware and glassware, and microwave ovens, which leak primarily through the oven's door if it does not seal tightly enough.

Nuclear medicine exposes more people to radiation than any other source. Although X rays have been used to diagnose various medical and dental problems for almost a century, some critics claim that X rays may be more harmful than helpful. The use of X-ray and similar machines must be carefully monitored to avoid the risk of exposing patients to more radiation than is necessary for diagnosis. Radioactive substances used for different types of diagnosis include iodine 131, to detect thyroid malfunctions, and barium, to view the digestive tract.

Electromagnetic radiation may also be a health hazard in homes. In July 1987, New York State health authorities published the results of the Power Line Research Project, a study on the possible effects of electromagnetic fields. The five-year project indicated that in homes with high electromagnetic fields resulting from nearby power-distribution lines, childhood cancer rates were double those in homes with lower electromagnetic fields. The study also showed that electromagnetic fields had behavioral and nervous system effects on lab animals, but they were not clearly considered hazardous. The study did not support claims that electromagnetic fields create genetic defects. Researchers concluded that electromagnetic fields definitely created biological effects, with principal concerns about cancer and secondary concerns about brain and behavioral changes.

Electromagnetic fields that come from television sets and VDTs for home computers and video games also may be a special threat to children, who are generally more sensitive to radiation than adults, yet tend to sit closer to these screens. Although the threat of electromagnetic fields remains a highly controversial topic, scientists suggest that those people who are concerned should try to live at least a half mile away from power lines.

While many questions remain about which objects and substances pose the greatest health risks, the wisest approach may be to avoid certain products. Meanwhile, the more people know about the contents of substances in their homes and offices, the more likely they will be to remain safe. Two general rules are: keep chemicals, particularly poisons, away from children; and do not smoke. If certain chemicals or cleansers prove to be less harmful than once thought, no harm has been done if people have used substitutes that are known to be safe now. The following chapter will explore other ways to prevent and possibly conquer environmental threats.

CHAPTER 7

WHERE TO START

Residents of New Jersey protest the construction of a toxic waste storage facility in their neighborhood.

Many business practices, government policies, and personal habits can cause environmental damage to the earth at large and to an individual in particular. Some of these dangers may seem overwhelming, but in order to change them, people must believe they can make a difference. The place to begin making changes is in each individual's day-to-day life. By recognizing small ways to help, more and more people can begin to protect and improve their own lives and the future of other life forms in the world around them.

Food Safety

The average American consumes approximately 10 pounds of chemical additives each year. Additives often are used to enhance the look and taste of products that actually offer no nutritional value and may even be harmful. These products may contain chemicals that the human body cannot safely absorb, and have the potential to cause a variety of ill effects. Diet-related illnesses include heart diseases, diabetes, and cancer of the stomach, breasts, and colon.

The local supermarket sells many products that contain chemical additives and preservatives. In addition, many products may use labeling that is confusing or deceptive. Packages marked with the words *100% natural* may include lard or meat products that contain chemicals. The words *naturally flavored* may refer to the flavoring used, while the main contents of the package may include additives. For example, *naturally flavored orange soda* may mean that the orange flavoring is natural, but allows the soda itself to contain artificial additives and preservatives.

Products defined as farm fresh or health foods may have healthy-sounding names, but these can be misleading unless the consumer checks the ingredients carefully. Other products emphasize which harmful elements they do *not* contain in order to play down their more harmful ingredients. Even products that seem fresher, such as fruit, vegetables, eggs, unpackaged bread, and fish, may contain additives and preservatives. Yet these products often do not have labels and therefore do not offer the consumer any warning about unhealthy ingredients.

Many common foods contain high amounts of sugar and fat and low amounts of fiber. Some basic health problems may be caused by popular, everyday flavorings such as sugar and salt. In addition to tooth decay, sugar has been linked to obesity and diabetes. Salt, which has been increasingly added to foods over recent decades, is considered the major source of hypertension, or high blood pressure, which leads to kidney failure, stroke, and heart disease. In contrast, nations where most people maintain low-salt diets report few cases of hypertension.

Among other common food offenders are artificial sweeteners, such as aspartame, which may affect the brain and cause epileptic seizures, and saccharin, which is linked to bladder cancer in animal tests. Cosmetic additives, used to make foods look more attractive, may cause cancer. Examples include Citrus Red No. 2, which is injected into the skin of some Florida oranges, and Red No. 3, which is used to color cherries, candy, and baked goods. Red No. 40, a dye used often in foods such as soft drinks, hot dogs, candy, pastry, and pet foods, has proven to cause cancer in mice. Certain preservatives, such as di-, tri-, and polyphosphates, used in foods such as hamburgers, sausages, processed meats and cheese, frozen chicken and pizza, and cookies and cakes, have proven to cause kidney damage in test animals.

One of the most common food additives is sodium nitrite, an artificial chemical first used to color foods and later found to prevent the growth of the bacteria that causes botulism, a potentially fatal type of food poisoning. However, in the 1960s researchers discovered that nitrites combine with the body's natural chemicals to form nitrosamines, some of the most powerful carcinogens yet discovered. Although the meat industry has reduced the use of nitrites dramatically in recent years, hot dogs and bacon continue to contain the substance. However, research shows that vitamin C helps to interfere with the process of nitrosamine formation in the stomach.

Of course, common sense allows that not all foods are entirely unhealthy, and hope remains that some foods may actually rectify negative effects. The additive BHA, a preservative added to cereals and baked goods, may help to inhibit the formation of cancer. Similarly, naturally occurring substances called indoles, which are found in vegetables such as broccoli, brussels sprouts, cabbage, cauliflower, and turnips, also seem to help weaken the process of cancer formation.

Indirect Additives

No matter how descriptive food labels are, some chemicals enter the food supply in ways that cannot be measured or recorded. Research

In Los Angeles, health officials dispose of cartons of tainted cheese responsible for the deaths of more than 30 people.

performed by the United States Department of Agriculture and the FDA indicates that meat and high-fat dairy products are more likely to be heavily contaminated by pesticides than other foods. Because the animals that supply these products are further along in the food chain, they accumulate all of the pesticides and radiation absorbed by various grasses, grains, and vegetables during their growing season.

Many meat and dairy products also contain antibiotics and hormones that farmers feed their livestock. By using these drugs, farmers can avoid disease and enhance growth in their livestock, while feeding them less grain and other food. Just as these additives accumulate at higher levels in livestock that are further along in the food chain, they, in turn, are passed along to the human body when people eat livestock containing high amounts of fat. Even without these additives, animal fats and cholesterol clearly are linked with heart disease.

Antibiotics are now fed to cattle and chickens throughout their lives. Antibiotics are drugs introduced to the body to fight disease, and their strength depends on whether the disease has developed a resistance to them. As the bacteria that cause disease encounter the antibiotic, they begin to build an immunity to the drug. When the body frequently encounters antibiotics, these drugs lose their ability to act strongly to fight disease. Unfortunately, the meat industry primarily uses the same two antibiotics commonly prescribed to humans: penicillin and tetracycline. Because humans are consuming many of these drugs through their regular diet, the antibiotics' effectiveness is weakened.

Harmful bacteria that have developed a resistance to antibiotics are referred to as resistance bacteria. Two well-known strains are clostridium, which causes tetanus, and salmonella, which causes paratyphoid and food poisoning. These fairly common diseases are becoming more difficult for doctors to fight because patients have consumed so many antibiotics through their diet. Although substitute antibiotics rarely used by humans have been suggested for use with livestock, drug companies and meat producers continue to use the traditional products with which they are familiar.

Food may also become contaminated from various sources during preparation. Salmonella bacteria are a common cause of food poisoning. Salmonella poisoning can be prevented by making sure that chicken and eggs are fully cooked. Also, be sure to wash carefully the utensils and surfaces that were used to prepare the chicken while it was raw.

Another food tip is to avoid the use of aluminum cookware. When cooking acidic foods, the aluminum can break down and produce toxic salts that eventually may lead to brain damage. Teflon and similar nonstick finishes may scratch and release plastic, a carcinogen, into foods.

Another source of food contamination involves the release of radiation from leaks in nuclear plants or dumps. If power stations are not secure from leakage, radioactive materials may enter the food chain. The major threat comes from fish, which thrive on contaminated plankton, and milk, which comes from cows that have eaten contaminated grass. This type of radiation in food results in the loss of essential minerals from the body, fatigue, headaches, and the loss of appetite.

Food Irradiation

In recent years more people have become aware of another type of radiation in food. A process called food irradiation uses radiation to preserve the shelf life of fresh food. Proponents of food irradiation argue that the gamma rays used in the process help to save food by slowing the process of ripening and by killing insects and bacteria. Opponents of this practice claim that it depletes food's nutritional value, hides bacterial contamination of foods that have begun to rot, and exposes consumers to carcinogens. According to the 1988 book *The Earth Report,* edited by Edward Goldsmith and Nicholas Hildyard, tests on rats show that irradiated foods lead to cancer, mutations, and genetic disorders.

Many of the most commonly irradiated foods are grains, vegetables, fruits, and spices—foods that traditionally have been considered healthier because they did not undergo high amounts of processing. In addition, pork is often irradiated, despite the fact that this type of meat is more likely to absorb ionizing radiation than other types of meat. For instance, pigs absorb six times more radiation than cows. Since

This St. Louis, Missouri, power plant was the first in the nation to burn garbage to produce electricity.

1986, when the Food and Drug Administration approved food irradiation, public concern has grown regarding its possible threat to public health. Many European countries have banned the practice of food irradiation, as have certain states in the United States. But new evidence is emerging that irradiation is safer then the pesticides and preservatives it replaces. The health issue remains to be resolved.

Water Safety

According to a 1988 study by the EPA, America's drinking water contains over 2,000 chemicals. When testing a number of public water systems that serve over 10,000 people, the EPA found that 45% contained volatile chemical compounds, including carcinogens. These figures are cause for concern, particularly because most water supplies have not even been tested for the possible threat of chemical contamination. In fact, the EPA checks regularly for less than 20 chemical pollutants, a limitation that allows the possibility of missing serious health threats.

For the average person, several methods can be used to check water for contaminants. Obvious signs of unclean water can be detected in the color, smell, and taste of tap water. Those concerned about tap water pollution should check with neighbors and local public water supplies to see how often and how thoroughly their water is tested. Another way to be certain of safe water is to mail tap water to a professional lab for analysis or to buy a home testing kit.

If a person is convinced that his or her water is unsafe, he or she can take several actions. In the short term, people can purchase a home drinking water treatment, such as a purifier or filter. Although bottled water can be purchased easily, at prices from 2 to 35 cents per glass, these products are not always safe. In fact, they are subject to less stringent safety standards than tap water. But short-term measures cannot replace the need to provide and maintain a clean water supply. Even without drinking tap water, people regularly absorb water through the skin, nose, and mouth while showering or swimming. The most effective way to safeguard a public water supply may be through the unified effort of neighbors who form and act through a community organization.

Creating Change

As individuals, people can take many actions in their day-to-day lives that will help make their environment healthier. A big part of this improvement requires learning how to change. Change begins with thinking differently in order to modify old, unhealthy habits. For example, people can work to create cleaner air by driving less and carpooling, walking, or riding bicycles whenever possible. They also can help decrease fossil fuel emissions by using fuel-efficient automobiles and public transportation.

Eating carefully can help the environment, as well as an individual's digestive and circulatory systems. People can improve their health and avoid overly processed foods by eating healthy foods such as vegetables and fruit rather than meat. Buying fresh foods from organic gardeners who do not use herbicides and pesticides is even healthier. This helps the environment by reducing the amount of harmful chemicals in the food chain. Consumers can even pressure fast-food chains to reduce excess packaging by eating at those chains that use less wasteful packaging.

Another way to create change that will help both people and the environment is to modify shopping habits. For example, millions of people use disposable plastic diapers that end up in local landfills. Using cloth diapers that can be washed and reused many times would greatly save landfill space. Similarly, purchasing products that use less packaging, such as bulk items, creates less litter. Other wise buys include products made of recycled materials and natural materials, such as wood and glass, rather than plastic.

In fact, recycling is one of the easiest and most effective ways to improve the environment. Much of what is now discarded as waste can be recycled. According to Dr. Paul Connnet in *Waste Management*, most materials are recyclable or reusable to varying degrees. He finds that recycling seems to work best when trash is sorted at the place it originates, that is, with the person who creates it.

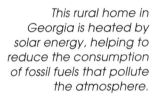

This rural home in Georgia is heated by solar energy, helping to reduce the consumption of fossil fuels that pollute the atmosphere.

Estimates show that between 20% and 88% of what people now throw away could be recycled. Indeed, some parts of Europe, Asia, and North America report recycling rates of over 65%. Countries that are more energy-conscious than the United States—Japan, West Germany, the Netherlands, and Italy, for instance—already recycle more than twice as much as the United States does. Japan recycled 50% of its

waste paper, 55% of its glass bottles, and 66% of its beverage and food cans in 1988. In 1986, United States residents recycled only 23% of their paper, 9% of their glass, and 25% of their aluminum products.

Once trash is sorted it can be handled in various ways. Most paper, which comprises approximately 40% of the waste, can be recycled, although certain contaminants may make some of it unusable. Newspapers contribute about 7% of the weight in municipal wastes and also comprise the most frequently recycled products. In 1987, about 36% of recycled newspapers were made into newsprint, 31% were converted to paperboard for packaging, and the remainder was used for construction materials such as roofing and insulation.

Aluminum is one of the most frequently used metals. Throwing away one aluminum can wastes as much energy as using a half gallon of gasoline. Beverage cans are easily melted and manufactured into identical new cans. Although about 50% of beverage cans were recycled in 1987, other types of aluminum are recycled less often. In contrast, cans made of tin and bimetal, which is made of tin with aluminum on the ends, are much more difficult to recycle. The mixture of metals contaminates the process of melting in a furnace. However, once a can is de-tinned, high-quality steel can be recycled.

Glass adds about 10 billion pounds to landfills annually. If collected carefully, bottles and jars can be washed and reused, but most are crushed, fed into furnaces, and melted to create new containers. Recycled glass can be used to make fiberglass, construction materials, road materials, abrasives, and—of course—new bottles and jars.

Plastic wastes are the subject of much controversy. Although they account for only 7% of municipal waste collections, they take up approximately 30% of space in landfills. However, recycling this material is especially difficult because there are many different types of plastic, yet they are all difficult to tell apart. Distinguishing between plastics is important in the process of reusing those materials. One approach to reducing the volume of plastic waste materials is to avoid buying products made of or packaged in plastic whenever possible.

Political Change

A major key to creating long-term environmental change is the involvement of local organizations. A group of people is usually more effective than a single individual at creating change because elected officials realize that they represent a number of votes. Once these leaders become aware that voters in their districts are concerned with issues, such as unsafe water supplies, curbside recycling programs, or public

Members of the next generation demonstrate in Washington, D.C., against the clear-cutting of national forests.

transit and agricultural reform, they are more likely to adopt this stance to win votes in their area. In this way, local groups can influence congresspeople to work to improve conditions that directly affect their community.

Many public service organizations work to create environmental change on both national and international levels. Most groups promote a specific cause. Individuals can contribute time and money to a group that supports a cause about which they feel strongly. For information about contacting various groups, check local libraries or look at the organizations listed in the back of this book.

Individuals also influence which issues get attention and how money is spent by writing to local leaders, representatives, senators, and even the president. Lists of officials and their addresses can be located at any library and often appear in newspapers. People can also write to newspapers to alert local officials and the public at large to the existence of unsafe environmental problems. As more people inform their leaders of their concern about environmental health, these officials may lead nationwide changes.

As more nations and individuals realize the value of clean air and water, they may all work together to improve the health of the earth and everyone on it. First, each individual must recognize his or her own value as a force for change. Every individual can create small changes through recycling and wise buying. As more people pursue these efforts, greater goals will be achieved. Just as every atom of polluted air collects in the earth, sky, and water to cause harm, every individual with positive efforts adds to a brighter future. Environmental hazards and health are shared, and chosen, by all.

APPENDIX:
FOR MORE INFORMATION

The following is a list of organizations and associations that can provide further information on the issues discussed in this book.

American Cancer Society
1599 Clifton Road, N.E.
Atlanta, GA 30329
(404) 320-3333

American College of Occupational
  and Environmental Medicine
55 West Seegers Road
Arlington Heights, IL 60005
(708) 228-6850

Citizen's Clearinghouse for
  Hazardous Waste
P.O. Box 926
Arlington, VA 22216
(703) 276-7070

Consumer Product Safety
  Commission
6 World Trade Center
New York, NY 10048
(212) 264-1125

Environmental Action Foundation
6930 Carroll Avenue, Suite 600
Takoma Park, MD 20912

Environmental Defense Fund
257 Park Avenue South
New York, NY 10010
(212) 505-2100

Environmental Protection Agency
401 M Street SW
Washington, DC 20460
(202) 382-2090

Friends of the Earth
218 D Street SE
Washington, DC 20003
(202) 544-2600

Greenpeace
1436 U Street NW
Washington, DC 20009
(202) 462-1177

National Coalition Against the
  Misuse of Pesticides
530 Seventh Street SE
Washington, DC 20003
(202) 543-5450

Natural Resources Defense Council
40 West 20th Street
New York, NY 10011
(212) 727-2700

Sierra Club
530 Bush Street
San Francisco, CA 94108
(415) 981-8634

Society for Occupational and
  Environmental Health
6728 Old McLean Village Drive
McLean, VA 22101
(703) 556-9222

U.S. Department of Agriculture
14th Street and Independence
  Avenue SW
Washington, DC 20250
(202) 447-2791

U.S. Public Interest Research Group
215 Pennsylvania Avenue SE
Washington, DC 20003
(202) 546-9707

FURTHER READING

Brodeur, Paul. *Currents of Death: Power Lines, Computer Terminals, and the Attempt To Cover Up Their Threat to Your Health.* New York: Simon & Schuster, 1989.

Corson, Walter H., ed. *The Global Ecology Handbook: What You Can Do About the Environmental Crisis.* Boston: Beacon Press, 1990.

Earthworks Group. *50 Simple Things You Can Do To Save the Earth.* Berkeley, CA: Earthworks Press, 1989.

Flaste, Richard, ed. *The New York Times Book of Science Literacy: What Everyone Needs To Know from Newton to the Knuckleball.* New York: Times Books/ Random House, 1991.

Gay, Kathlyn. *Silent Killers: Radon and Other Hazards.* New York: Franklin Watts, 1988.

Goldman, Benjamin A. *The Truth About Where You Live: An Atlas for Action on Toxins and Mortality.* New York: Times Books/Random House, 1991.

Kime, Robert E., *Environment and Health.* Guilford, CT: Dushkin Publishing Group, 1992.

Naar, Jon. *Design for a Livable Planet: How You Can Help Clean up the Environment.* New York: Harper & Row, 1990.

Null, Gary. *Clearer, Cleaner, Safer, Greener: A Blueprint for Detoxifying Your Environment.* New York: Villard Books, 1990.

Porritt, Jonathan, ed. *Save the Earth.* Atlanta, GA: Turner, 1991.

Pringle, Laurence. *Lives at Stake: The Science and Politics of Environmental Health.* New York: Macmillan, 1980.

Wax, Nina. *Occupational Health.* New York: Chelsea House, 1994.

Winter, Ruth. *A Consumer's Dictionary of Household, Yard, and Office Chemicals.* New York: Crown, 1992.

GLOSSARY

acid deposition excessively acidic precipitation in the form of rain, snow, sleet, fog, or dry particles; caused by atmospheric pollutants such as nitrogen oxide and sulfur oxide

asbestos any of several minerals used in making insulation; crumbling asbestos releases fibers that can become airborne and cause lung disease and cancer if inhaled

cancer any malignant tumor that destroys normal tissue as it spreads to adjacent tissue layers or to other parts of the body

carcinogen a cancer-causing substance or agent

ecosystem an area in which species interact with and are interdependent upon each other and their environment

electromagnetic field a combination of electrical and magnetic energy given off by electrical appliances such as computers and power lines

formaldehyde a chemical substance found in particle board and many glues, paints, fabrics, and surface coatings; it can cause irritation of the eyes, lungs, and skin, and has been found to cause cancer in laboratory animals

fossil fuels combustible materials, such as coal, oil, and natural gas, formed from the remains of plants and animals over millions of years and under conditions of high temperature and pressure

global warming the gradual increase of the earth's temperature as a result of heat trapped by atmospheric pollutants

greenhouse effect the trapping of infrared radiation in the earth's atmosphere by gases such as carbon dioxide

groundwater water beneath the earth's surface that flows slowly between soil and rock, and that supplies wells and springs

landfill a site where garbage is dumped, compacted, and covered with a thin layer of earth

lead a toxic metallic element that can accumulate in the body and damage internal organs

ozone a relatively unstable form of oxygen containing three oxygen atoms instead of two; at ground level, ozone is an irritating form of air pollution, but at higher levels it forms a layer in the atmosphere that screens out harmful solar radiation

passive smoking the inhalation of tobacco smoke produced by another person's smoking of cigarettes, cigars, or pipes; also referred to as secondhand smoking

radiation particles and rays emitted from atomic matter; radiation can be nonionizing (not harmful to living creatures) or ionizing (damaging to living tissue), depending on its energy level

sewage refuse liquids or waste matter

wetlands land or areas, such as tidal flats or swamps, containing much soil moisture

INDEX

LaVonne Carlson-Finnerty is the author of two books in the Encyclopedia of Health series, *Memory and Learning* and *Environmental Health*. She has edited six books in the series, including *Suicide, Sleep, Pain, Anxiety and Phobias, Juvenile Delinquency,* and *Medical Diagnosis*. She is now an editor at Outlet Book Company, a division of Random House. While a student at the University of Texas, LaVonne worked with biologists and ecologists on research projects in California, Mexico, and Venezuela.

Dale C. Garell, M.D., is medical director of California Children Services, Department of Health Services, County of Los Angeles. He is also associate dean for curriculum at the University of Southern California School of Medicine and clinical professor in the Department of Pediatrics & Family Medicine at the University of Southern California School of Medicine. From 1963 to 1974, he was medical director of the Division of Adolescent Medicine at Children's Hospital in Los Angeles. Dr. Garell has served as president of the Society for Adolescent Medicine, chairman of the youth committee of the American Academy of Pediatrics, and as a forum member of the White House Conference on Children (1970) and White House Conference on Youth (1971). He has also been a member of the editorial board of the *American Journal of Diseases of Children*.

C. Everett Koop, M.D., Sc.D., is former Surgeon General, deputy assistant secretary for health, and director of the Office of International Health of the U.S. Public Health Service. A pediatric surgeon with an international reputation, he was previously surgeon-in-chief of Children's Hospital of Philadelphia and professor of pediatric surgery and pediatrics at the University of Pennsylvania. Dr. Koop is the author of more than 175 articles and books on the practice of medicine. He has served as surgery editor of the *Journal of Clinical Pediatrics* and editor-in-chief of the *Journal of Pediatric Surgery*. Dr. Koop has received nine honorary degrees and numerous other awards, including the Denis Brown Gold Medal of the British Association of Paediatric Surgeons, the William E. Ladd Gold Medal of the American Academy of Pediatrics, and the Copernicus Medal of the Surgical Society of Poland. He is a chevalier of the French Legion of Honor and a member of the Royal College of Surgeons, London.

PICTURE CREDITS